Teach Like a Prepper

Teach Like a Prepper

Be as Ready for Your First Day of School as You Are for the Zombie Apocalypse

Donald J. Pierce

ROWMAN & LITTLEFIELD
Lanham • Boulder • New York • London

Published by Rowman & Littlefield
An imprint of The Rowman & Littlefield Publishing Group, Inc.
4501 Forbes Boulevard, Suite 200, Lanham, Maryland 20706
www.rowman.com

86-90 Paul Street, London EC2A 4NE, United Kingdom

Copyright © 2022 by Donald J. Pierce

All rights reserved. No part of this book may be reproduced in any form or by any electronic or mechanical means, including information storage and retrieval systems, without written permission from the publisher, except by a reviewer who may quote passages in a review.

British Library Cataloguing in Publication Information Available

Library of Congress Cataloging-in-Publication Data

Names: Pierce, Donald J., 1981– author.
Title: Teach like a prepper : be as ready for your first day of school as you are for the zombie apocalypse / Donald J. Pierce.
Description: Lanham, Maryland : Rowman & Littlefield, 2022. | Summary: "Donald J. Pierce is a military veteran, as well as a veteran of the educational system. He has worked as a childcare provider, teacher, and school administrator over the span of his career"—Provided by publisher.
Identifiers: LCCN 2021037539 (print) | LCCN 2021037540 (ebook) | ISBN 9781475863826 (cloth) | ISBN 9781475863833 (paperback) | ISBN 9781475863840 (epub)
Subjects: LCSH: Classrooms—Planning. | Classroom management.
Classification: LCC LB3325.C5 P54 2022 (print) | LCC LB3325.C5 (ebook) | DDC 371.102/4—dc23
LC record available at https://lccn.loc.gov/2021037539
LC ebook record available at https://lccn.loc.gov/2021037540

*This book is dedicated to my daughter, Savannah.
She is the reason I am a prepper. I prepare
for the worst situations I can imagine so that
I can protect the best person I know.*

Contents

Introduction ix

1 Home Base 1
2 Supplies 17
3 Emergency Procedures 29
4 Classroom Management 41
5 The Substitute 55
6 Getting to Work and Back 61
7 Recycle and Reuse 71
8 Conclusion 77

About the Author 79

Introduction

It's the moment you have been dreading for months. You're sitting down at your desk to eat your breakfast and the peace and silence of the moment is broken by a clanking of bells. You have been planning and practicing for this moment. You've spent years studying and honing your skills for this day. You have hoarded and stockpiled your supplies. You thought you were ready, but the moment the bells start to ring a wave of dread washes over you. You know that the perimeter has now been breached and that they will soon be upon you. You can hear their voices as they make their way down the hallway to your location. The reality of the situation finally hits you. This is no dream. It is really the first day of school. Will you survive?

If you are reading this book, then you may be a prepper already, are thinking about becoming a prepper, or you are thinking that the prepper's mindset might work for you as an educator. So let us get down to the nitty-gritty. What exactly is a prepper? Preppers are individuals who actively prepare for all types of situations. They acquire resources such as emergency medical supplies, food and water, and tools, as well as learn new skills that can help them cope with many situations that may arise in an emergency. As a teacher, you do not necessarily need to prepare your classroom for the zombie apocalypse, but by using the prepper mindset you can be better prepared for when the unexpected occurs.

I have an analogy I like to use for being a teacher at a school. Teachers are like an island that is part of a chain of islands. You are connected deep down to the other educators on your campus. Your neighbor islands want to be there for you just as you want to be there for them. However, just like living on an island, you have to be able to find for yourself most of the time. It may take a while for your neighbors to get assistance to you if and when you need it. Teachers have their own classes to teach and administrators are often engaged in the day-to-day running of the school or are off campus at the district office. You have to be able to survive until help arrives. That is what this book is meant to help you do. It is designed to show you how to be prepared and be able to help yourself and your students when there is no one available to lend you a hand.

Being mentally prepared to be a prepper is very important. The art of prepping is a mindset as much as it is a lifestyle. Like most aspects of your life, prepping comes down to your ability to make choices and adapt to new situations. Every day, we are beset with problems that we must solve in order to continue with our daily lives. To start thinking

Figure 0.1 A Lockdown Drill. *Author's daughter, eight years old.*

the "prepper way," here are a few common pepper sayings for you to think about.

(1) *Murphy's Law: Anything that can go wrong will go wrong.* This means that you should be ready for anything.
(2) *Two is one and one is none.* This means that you should always have a back to every item and system you use.
(3) *Always be ready to improvise, adapt, and overcome.* You should accept that you will need to make changes at the spur of the moment.
(4) *No matter what happens, you can survive it.* This simply means that no matter the odds and no matter the challenge, you can get through it.

Note: Please check with your school district on restrictions before implementing the ideas presented in this book. They may not allow certain items, have regulations on classroom layouts, or restrict/require certain rules that you can have for your classroom and students.

Chapter 1

Home Base

It doesn't matter if your home base is a classroom, a cabin in the woods, or an underground bunker. Every prepper knows that you need a base of operation from which to work from. This is where you will make your plans, organize your gear, store your supplies, and spend the majority of your time. If you are a teacher, then that place will normally be your classroom. As an educator, you probably spend about 6 to 10 hours a day, 5 days a week, 220 days a year in your classroom. It is like a second home to many educational professionals.

You are there before school begins getting your lessons in order and praying that you get to use that single copy machine that is working in the teacher work room. You are there from when the first bell rings until the bell for lunch goes off filling the minds of your students with essential knowledge. You probably spend more than a few lunch periods grading papers and getting the afternoon's lessons ready.

After lunch, you spend the afternoon keeping those youths awake while continuing to fill their heads with the valuable information they will need to be successful in life. Finally, after the last bell of the day has rung, you will probably spend an hour or two grading more papers than you remember assigning, straightening up the classroom, attending a meeting (committee, department, or grade level), and generally trying to get yourself physically and mentally ready for the next school day.

The point is that, as a teacher, you will spend a good part of your professional adult life in your classroom. You probably spend more time in your classroom than you do your own home. That is why it will be the perfect spot for your home base. Since it is your base of operations, you need to prepare your classroom not only for teaching your students valuable information and skills but also for being able to take care of them and yourself when you are there.

Remember that your safety and your sanity is just as important as that of your young charges. That is why the layout of your classroom is so important. A chaotic classroom leads to a chaotic group of students and reduces your ability to handle emergency situations when they arise. Always remember that as a teacher, you set the tone for the class. You are the one the students will look to for leadership when things go wrong. And as we all know, in the education field, things are always going wrong.

DECORATIONS

It can be said that a classroom is truly a reflection of its teacher's personality. Teachers are well-known for their ability to turn an empty room into a place that feels like a second home to their students as well as to themselves. The way an educator does this is by creating an atmosphere in their room that is welcoming in nature yet encourages their students' learning. This is no easy task by any stretch of the imagination, but it is possible and many teachers do this every school year.

An important thing to know when teaching like a prepper is that heavily decorated classrooms are a big no-no. Don't do it. Heavily decorated classrooms have been found to effect students by bombarding them with too much visual stimulation. This bombardment can interfere with a student's ability to focus on their lessons as well as the student's ability to retain any information presented to them.

Think of it like this, you are standing in a room with forty television sets all going at the same time and all of them on a different channel. Even if you try your hardest to focus on one of the televisions, the noise and flashing images of the other televisions will constantly be distracting you. This is exactly what it is like for students in a room with an excessive amount of decorations in it. It is overwhelming for them. A good prepper knows that, more often than not, less is more. A good prepper knows that even if you have very little to work with or use, you can make what you do have on hand go a long way and do some really amazing things. A little creativity and ingenuity can go a long way in regards to decorations.

In prepping, preppers are encouraged to select and gather a collection of tools and equipment that are multifunctional. This means that these are items are designed to or can easily serve more than one purpose. Items that are reusable and durable are highly prized in the prepper community. For example, a good, solid multitool is highly valued by many preppers. It is capable of replacing a dozen or more tools and can often be carried in a pant's pocket or purse without hindering the carrier.

Now this does not mean that teachers cannot have a beautiful selection of colors and imagery throughout their classroom. In fact, it is the colors and collection of decorations that turn a drab room into a place of learning that has a homey feel to it. It just means that a teacher needs to choose decorations that are both functional and fun to behold. A good example of this are educational posters. We have all seen them and most of us love them. For those unfamiliar with these particular posters, they present information about a topic or show the steps need to perform an action for a variety of subjects. These posters are often very colorful and have great imagery. The best part is that often you can collect posters that have a theme to them. I once used posters with a super-hero theme to show different math topics. The kids love the imagery and the posters served as reminders to the students on how to solve equations.

Another great decoration for classrooms that serve multiple purposes are maps. Anyone who has taught before knows that you will often discuss places located all around the world. Unfortunately, we live in a world where the knowledge of geographical locations has been severely diminished. Students are unaware of the locations of many countries and major cities. There are even high school students in the United States that cannot tell you where major cities, monuments, and geographical features of the United States are located. A large map can help you to show the students where the places you are discussing are actually located. I can tell you that I used to have a massive map of the world on my wall and I found uses for it in almost every subject. My students could often be found looking at my map trying to find locations that I mentioned during a particular lesson. It is also useful for teaching the students map-reading skills (it is never too early to teach children basic survival skills). Think about how many grown adults can't properly read a map or know how to use a compass.

There are many educational items that you, as an educator, can hang on your walls or place on your shelves that will brighten up a room and help educate the children at the same time. Don't forget, you can switch out your room's decorations at anytime you wish. You can make changes based on the time of the year or on new concepts being taught.

An item I used often was a pocket chart. This may seem old-fashioned, but I found them invaluable. All you need to do is display the information on sentence strips or notecards and then slide them into the clear pockets. They can be used to display vocabulary words, math problems that need to be copied down, or even announcements about upcoming events. These take up very little space and can be used for multiple subjects. As I stated before, multifunctional items are very important when you are trying to thinking like a prepper.

In addition to educational materials, there are other items that can serve multiple purposes and make great decorations. Stuffed animals are great for decorating a classroom, but also they are great for calming down or comforting upset children. You'll even find that older students like to hug them when they are feeling down. Posters with classroom or school rules on them remind students of what is expected of them (more on that later). Sheets, blankets, and tapestries make great backdrops, wall decorations, and curtains for classrooms. They can also be used when the heat goes out and the students start to get cold. If you have ever taught somewhere when the heaters stop working and the temperature starts to drop, then you know a good blanket is a lifesaver.

Finally on decorating, do not forget to add a bit of yourself to the classroom. Banners and flags of your favorite sports teams, college pennants, animal posters, or whatever you like are not only decorative, but tell the students about who you are as a person. They will help the students to become more comfortable with who you are and can even help you open up a dialogue with students. Maybe they like the same sports team or share a love of a certain book that you do. Just remember that your decorations should be age and school appropriate. No matter how much you love zombie films and television shows, you shouldn't hang posters of zombies eating people's brains around your first-grade classroom.

ORGANIZATION

Being well-organized is something that probably seems obvious to most people. On a daily basis, teachers manage anywhere from 24 to 240 students each semester. You are probably wondering why this would even be included in this book if it is such an obvious thing. The reason it is included it is because it is so vitally important to the functioning of a classroom that it needs to be mentioned and explored.

Now, I will be the first to admit that I am not the most organized person in the world. However, when I started my teaching career, I was very determined to keep a very neat and organized classroom and have a tidy teacher's desk. It is quite possible that a neat teacher's desk is the Holy Grail of education. For a short time, I was semi-successful. However, as that first school year progressed, I found the goal of maintaining tidiness getting harder and harder to reach. As any teacher can tell you, it is not always easy to keep a neat and organized classroom. The essays and worksheets that you need to grade start to pile up quickly and the stack of papers you need to return gets larger and larger with each passing day.

However, there are lots of ways to keep a classroom organized enough that you can find what you need when you need it and I learned them quickly, even if it was the hard way. As a prepper, it is vital that you know where all your important gear is at all times. The first step to maintaining an organized classroom/home base is to allocate your storage areas accordingly. Depending on the layout or your classroom, you may have a lot of cabinets and shelves, you may have only one or two book shelves, or you may even have nothing but your desk drawers. Fear not though, because it is possible to be organized even with very little storage space. The key to it is looking for alternative places to store your goods that you never thought to look at before. Let us start with cabinets.

Cabinets are a wonderful way to keeping your supplies not only organized but also secure. Cabinets are perfect for storing those items that are not only unsafe for the students to get their hands on like chemicals, tools, and sharp objects but also the supplies that seem to wander away on their own whenever you leave the classroom. Have you ever noticed how every time your leave your classroom, some highly prized or valued items like white printer paper just seem to disappear? It is almost as though they have decided to get up and go for a walk all on their own.

Having cabinets and securing them can help prevent any unauthorized field trips by your most precious supplies.

As far as cabinets go, they come in two basic flavors. There are the cabinets that can be locked and the cabinets that have no way of being secured. Obviously, most teachers and preppers prefer the style of cabinets that can be locked. These kinds of cabinets prevent highly valuable items from getting up and walking away on their own or dangerous item from getting into the wrong hands. However, if you are unlucky enough to have the kind of cabinetry that cannot be easily secured, you do have a few options available to you.

The first option is to have locks installed. You will need your administration's permission to do this, but if you can convince them of the importance of having locks on your cabinets, they may just acquiesce to your request. Trust me, you will not be sorry if you can lock your cabinets (unless you lose the keys that is). If you teach any subject that involves the use of chemicals, flammable materials, or other such volatile items, then your administration will be more likely to install locks. Hint: If you are required to maintain a supply of cleaning products, then most states require that those items are stored securely away from students. Check your local laws about how certain items are required to be stored. Your administration can't deny you lock if it is the law.

The second option is to put child-proofing locks on the cabinets yourselves. This may seem silly, but they really work. Think about how many adults struggle to operate child-proofing devices even if they were the ones to install them. There is a reason comedy shows have skits involving an adult trying to open a fridge or toilet that is child-proofed. Some of the locks are actually really difficult to undo. These locks not only prevent smaller children from being able to open the cabinets but also deter thieves. The reason that these devices are a deterrent is because they create an obstacle and add time to the process of stealing. Most thieves want to be able to just grab and go. By creating even small obstacles and adding time for the would-be thief to be found out, you reduce the likelihood of a theft actually occurring.

A third option available to you is to install an alarm on the shelves. Many thrift stores and hardware stores carry window alarms. These work by using a reed switch and a magnet. The reed switch attaches to your window frame while the magnet attaches to the actual window. When the window is opened, the magnet pulls away from the reed switch and the alarm will go off. This continues until the window is closed again. I like these because they are cheap and the sound scares away the would-be thieves. Attach the reed switch to one cabinet and the magnet to the other. Boom! You have an alarm system that everyone within twenty-five years of your classroom will hear. Just remember to turn off the alarm before you open the cabinet or you will scare your students and your neighbors. FYI: I happen to know firsthand that the alarm can be used to awaken any students who may have drifted off to sleep during your lesson.

When deciding what goes into the cabinets, it is best to prioritize your supplies based on their danger to other peoples and/or their value to others. Dangerous items should obviously be put out of the reach of students. A good prepper keeps their most valuable items somewhere that looters can't find them. They try to think like a thief so they can protect their most important resources. That is why valuables should not only be placed in the cabinets but be hidden among less valuable items. We will discuss this more in detail later on.

The next type of storage unit that we will discuss are shelves. Whether it is a wooden book shelf, steel industrial shelving, or a wall-mounted decorative shelf it does not matter. They are all equally useful. I always dedicate each of my shelves to a singular purpose for easy for organization. One of the most effective ways to utilize shelves is to have dedicated shelves for student books, one for your personal books, another one for notebooks, another for manipulatives that you would use for math lessons, and perhaps one for science materials. By dedicating a shelf to a singular type of item or subject materials, you reduce the risk of overcrowding or getting confused where an item is located or where it should be returned to when you are done using it. It will also make it easier for students to locate items if you want them to gather any materials for you.

A good tip for getting the most out of your shelving units is to adjust the shelves' height based on the height of the items you plan to put on them. By doing this, you maximize the amount of space you have and ensure you can get as many supplies on there as possible. Most shelves are easily adjustable. Often you only need to lift the actual shelf up and move the tabs that stabilize it up or down. Even those shelving units which are not designed to be altered or easily altered can be adjusted with the help of a drill and a few screws. You can even add additional shelves by making them out of pressed particleboard or wood. Preppers are well-known for their ingenuity and ability to jerry-rig what we need.

So do not be afraid to be creative. Remember the old military adage of improvise, overcome, and adapt to survive.

Hypothetically, let us say that you are one of those unlucky individuals who gets to their new classroom and finds that there are no cabinets and maybe one bookcase. I've been there and I know the feeling of emptiness that washes over you when you see a room devoid of furniture other than student desks. Fear not, there are options available to you. Preppers know that the ability to adapt to situation is vital to survival. You have lots of options available and many of them will cost you little to no money.

The obvious choice is to ask your administration for the furniture you want. Now I know that getting items, especially, furniture from your school's leadership can be like tilting at windmills. So let us assume that you asked your administrators and even said "pretty pretty please with cherries on top," but that it did not bear any fruits. So let us focus on what we can do if you cannot get any storage units from your district.

One option is to utilize organizers that are designed for offices and classrooms. These include hanging organizers that can be hung from the walls around you classroom. These can be either the ones purchased in stores with room in each pocket to hold a file folder or homemade ones that can accommodate almost anything you need to store. You can even make your own by sewing pockets onto an old comforter and hanging it from the wall. Another option is to utilize stackable trays. These work great for organizing student papers and handouts you need to distribute. These take up very little space and you can safely stack them up to six trays high. A bonus is that they can be easily labeled so you do not forget what papers go where. This makes them great for student turn-in bins.

Another option you can think about is to obtain milk crates. Milk crates stack easily and can hold quite a bit of gear. You can also use them to hold files by utilizing hanging file folders. If you want a cheap source of these, check with local grocery and convenient stores. I have found many of them willing to give you a few when you tell them it is for your classroom. An alternative to milk crates are wine crates. All you need to do is paint over the alcohol references on the crate and you have a fashionable wooden storage unit.

If you are dead set on having traditional shelves, then you have the option to purchase inexpensive shelving units yourself. I have found many stores carry plastic shelving units that you assemble yourself for prices ranging from $20 to $60 for a four-tier shelf. In addition, you can go to the local thrift store or charity organization's store and find shelves of different styles and sizes for low prices. Most of the time, these second-hand units just need a touch of paint and a tightening of a few screws to look presentable. One last option is to go by large stores and see if they have shelving or displays in the back they intend to dispose of. I have got a few good things that way.

DESKS AND TABLES

Now we get to the placement of your desks and/or tables. There are many theories out there about how to arrange your students' desks. From a prepper's point of view, there are two important rules for the placement of desks/tables in your home base. These first of these rules is to maintain maneuverability throughout the classroom. As an educator, you need to be able to move from desk to desk to help your students and keep an eye on their progress. Ensure that you can get to any student or any place in the classroom easily.

The second rule is to maximize space allocation in your classroom. A classroom is a finite space and has limitations on how many desks and how many people can safely take up residence there at any given time. You need to ensure that you have enough room in your classroom for all your students to fit comfortably, for you to be able to move about, and for you to be able to house your equipment and tools of the trade. This can sometimes be a challenge. I once worked in a school as a middle school social studies teacher where I had six classes each day and forty students in each class. I had to learn to be creative with space to accommodate all those bodies and still be able to move about freely.

Thought observations, experimentation, and by own my experience, I have found two desk formations that work well from the prepper's point of view. Both of these formations emphasize the concepts I mentioned previously about ensuring teacher mobility and maximizing your space allocation. Not only do these formations ensure that you can easily get to each and every student when you need to, but they also allow you to fit a large number of students into a small space. A third advantage of these formations is that they can be altered at anytime to quite easily which make the formations flexible. This is a trait prepper's love.

10   *Chapter 1*

The first of these desk arrangements is based on the idea that you want students to be able to work together. The teacher forms up the desks in groups of four or five and then places these groups in columns of two or three. This allows the students to work with their peers if that is your style of teaching. A benefit of the groupings is that it allows students to help each other and have group discussions. It also has the added benefit of letting table groups compete against each other. I found that this leads to team building and creates a healthy competition in the classroom. The groups can easily be broken up into rows just by turning a few desks. This works best for examinations since it reduces the chance of students "accidentally" looking at their neighbor's test. Figure 1.1 shows that the teacher's desk is located in the rear of the classroom. This prevents students from easily walking by it and also allows the teacher to be able to see the entire class and the entrance clearly.

Front of the Class

XX	XX	XX
XX	XX	XX
X	X	X
XX	XX	XX
XX	XX	XX
X	X	X

Teacher's Desk

Figure 1.1   Diagram 1. *Source: Author created.*

The second formation is a personal favorite of mine for working with older students. It is the basic U-shaped formation. This formation works best when you have rectangular tables instead of the standard student desks, but desks can be used too if that is what you have to work with. In this configuration, the teacher will arrange the tables end to end (lengthwise). The chairs are aligned on both sides of the table so the students are facing each other and if they turn their heads in a 45-degree angle, they will be able to see the whiteboard/chalkboard/smart board at the front of the classroom. The table(s) that make up the bottom of the "U" will only have chairs on one side and they will be facing the front of the classroom.

If you have desks instead of chairs, then the desks on the sides of the "U" are facing inward. This, like with tables, will have the students facing toward each other. The teacher then has the bottom of the "U" as a single row of desks face the front of the classroom just as it did with the chairs. This shape allows you to stand in the center of the "U" and be able to see and reach each student easily. In this formation the teacher's desk is also in the back of the classroom for the same reasons as mentioned earlier (see figure 1.2).

Figures 1.1 and 1.2 show how to set up the desks in these two formations mentioned previously. When you look at the diagrams, you will notice that all the desks can easily see the front of the classroom and each desk is easily reachable. In the diagrams, each "X" represents a student's location whether in a desk or at a table.

THE TEACHER'S DESK

Now that you have your classroom decorated, your storage areas set up, and the students' desks arranged, it is time to set up your own desk to work from. A teacher's desk is a very personal and private spot in a classroom. It is sacred ground for teachers. Here is where your most personal items are kept. This is where your family photos are displayed, your teacher's computer is perched, and your student's assignments are graded. This is as personal a spot as your bedroom at home. It is also the thing that visitors often see, where you sit during parent–teacher conferences, and the spot in the classroom that tells other about what kind of person you are.

Chapter 1

Figure 1.2 **Diagram 2.** *Source: Author created.*

To keep your desk organized and secure there are a few tricks that preppers like to use that can easily translate to the educational career field. The first is to designate your desk drawers so that each drawer is used to store specific items. This goes along with the organization concepts discussed previously. Most teacher's desks have three drawers. Two medium-sized drawers on one side of the desk and one long, narrow drawer in the center of the desk. To do this you will need to decide what items need to be secured and what items need to be hidden from prying eyes and stick fingers.

The narrow center drawer is a great place for us to begin. This drawer is not only semi-concealed because of its location where the person sitting at the desk puts their legs and also the fact that it is recessed just behind the edge of the desk, but this drawer is also the most annoying of the drawers for people to open. Often the drawer is prevented from opening completely by the body of the person sitting in front of it or the desk chair. That is why I recommend placing smaller items that you do not need to have access to as often in this drawer. Flash drives, letter openers, multitools, and important papers and files. The reason I include important documents in this list is because you do not want those in a file cabinet that does not lock where anyone can read them. In addition, I place any valuable items in this drawer as well. Because it is the hardest of the drawers to access, it makes it more difficult for people to take things out of it easily and quickly. If I remove my wallet, keys, and phone, this is where they are stored.

   The two side drawers are broken into an equipment drawer and a documents drawer. In the top drawer, which is often the smaller of the two, you place one of your staplers, a box of staples, a box of paper clips, one box of each type of pens and markers, and other items you use on a daily basis. This makes it easy for you to get the gear you need. You will not be storing these on your desk, but rather in the drawer until they are needed. This reduces theft of your goods. When you notice that any of the items are running low, you go to your storage area and replenish your supply. The reason you only put one of each item in the drawer is so that the drawers does not get over crowded and messy, in addition to limiting the number of items available to be stolen.

   The bottom drawer should be designated for paperwork. This will be where you keep you student records, special needs paper work, new student packets, student/staff handbooks, and paper copies of students' grades. Using hanging file folders to organize these items and ordering their placement by category makes it even easier to find the right forms quickly. Now, behind these files is where you will hide your personal hygiene items. Ever teacher I have ever met keeps spare deodorant, toothbrush and toothpaste, mouthwash, hair brush, and similar items in their classroom. I like to keep these items out of the reach and sight of others, especially my students. That is why hiding them behind files works so well. In addition, you can hide any money you collected, your purse/wallet, or any other items in the same spot.

COMMUNICATION

As any prepper, soldier, or first responder can tell you, information is vital. When something happens you need to be able to know what is going on and what is being expected of you at a moment's notice. You might need to be able to communicate with those in charge and those who can best help you. Perhaps a lockdown has been announced and you need to know why or maybe a student vomited in your classroom and you need a member of the custodial staff to come clean it up. There are five types of communication methods commonly found that may be present in your classroom. If you are lucky, you will have more than one to rely on. These methods are telephones/cell phones, email/instant messages, intercom system, radios, and student runners. Let us examine these methods closer.

Telephones and cell phones are the most common form of communication in the classroom. In the past, most classrooms had a landline telephone set up so that the front office could communicate with the various classrooms and offices on campus. If you have one of these landline phones, I recommend that you keep a list of important phone numbers next to it. I would have the numbers printed large and have them labeled. These contacts should include, but are not limited to, the front office, attendance, school administration, and the nurse's office. If you do not have a classroom telephone, then your cell phone will have to suffice. You should have the phone number for the front office and administration in your cell phone no matter what. Not only in case you need to call for assistance, but also if you need to call out sick or to inform them that you will be late for work. In addition, keep the aforementioned list of important phone numbers posted near your desk where you will also keep a charger for your cell phone.

Email is the next most used form of communication and is quickly becoming the most common. Many school districts are relying more and more on email as their primary way of sharing email with their staff members. In addition to the school district offices, school administrators are now using emails to notify staff members of up common events, schedule meetings, and distribute messages that need to be shared with the student body. In regards to their usefulness, emails are fine for sending messages that are not a priority. However, unless the teachers are constantly monitoring their email account(s), important or time-sensitive information may not be relayed in a timely manner. A style of communication that is similar to email is instant messaging. Instant messaging is better for shorter messages and often quicker than emails. If you need to communicate with someone about a topic that is time sensitive, then using another means such as a telephone or radio is much quicker and I would recommend it over using email. Think about how often some people check their emails. Oddly enough, school districts do not want their teachers checking their emails during class time, yet school administrators get irritated when staff members do not reply to an email quickly.

The school-wide intercom system is a dying means of communication within modern-day schools. While some of these systems are two-way, most of them are one directional and teachers are only able to receive messages. Many educators dislike the fact that announcements made over the system interrupt their classes while they are trying to teach. I even know a teacher who "accidentally" disconnected the intercom speaker in their room. However, these devices do serve a purpose. When it comes to sending a message quickly across the entire campus, there are few other means of doing so that are as quick and thorough.

Radios are the next form of communication available to educators and a personal favorite of mine. Preppers often use radios to keep in contact with each other. Either using an amateur radio system (HAM radios) or handheld walkie-talkies, these radios defiantly serve a purpose when it comes to school-wide communication. More often than not, these types of radios are used only by administration, security, and maintenance/custodial staff members to alert them to an issue that need immediate attention. However, there are some schools that do issue them to all of their staff members so they can stay in contact even while moving about the campus or while on duty. If your school does not use radios, I recommend buying your own handheld radios. They are relatively inexpensive and very handy. I used to give one to each of my grade-level teammates so we could communicate with each other without needing to call over the phone or send an email. They were a lifesaver to have while on lunch duty. If there was a problem, I could call one of them over and inform them of the details and request assistance if needed, much better than yelling across the campus at someone and hoping that they hear you over the crowds of students.

The final method of communication available to educators is the student runner. The student runner is a trusted member of your class who knows their way around the campus and is reliable enough to be able to go from point A to point B without getting distracted or lost. These students are great for sending up attendance sheets, delivering items to other classrooms, and even fetching a staff member that you cannot reach for one reason or another. Student runners should defiantly not be your primary means of communication and should never be used in an emergency or lockdown situation. Using them in these circumstances can endanger the student as well as jeopardize your career.

As a final note on communications, I think that it is a good idea to have an AM/FM radio handy. Yes, I know this is "old-fashioned" technology. However, I think they are not only useful, but vital because communication also encompasses the ability to stay aware of local news and important information. If there is a natural weather occurrence or an event that will affect traffic, it is important that you know about it. I know that in the age of smartphones, this type of technology may seem antiquated, but from a prepper's point of view, cell phones run out of power or they may not get reception where you are located. Having even a pocket-sized radio can give you vital information that you need to prepare for whatever is coming your way.

No matter which forms of communication you have at your disposal or chose to use, ensure that you equipment is kept in good working order. In addition, you should also keep spare parts and multiple ways to keep your devices powered available with your gear. This includes, but is not limited to, cell phone chargers, laptop chargers, spare batteries, and even a portable solar charger.

Chapter 2

Supplies

Gear and supplies are a favorite topic among preppers. Preppers love talking about their gear more than conspiracy theorists love talking about the Illuminati and who actually shot John F. Kennedy. Most preppers cannot get enough of the newest gear and technology. If you are a prepper or know someone who is, then you probably have seen the smile that appears on their face when they go to the sporting goods store or the military surplus store. Preppers love to have the coolest gadgets and the best pieces of equipment. In this chapter, we will discuss the kinds of gear and supplies you will want to keep in your classroom. As an educator, I understand that teachers do not have a lot, if any, additional funds to spend on supplies. That is why my lists are made up of items that are inexpensive.

This is by no means a complete listing of what you may want to stockpile, but it will give you a good starting place and help get you into the right train of thought. I will be breaking the gear into seven categories: School Supplies, Gear and Tools, Custodial/Maintenance, First Aid, Lockdown Buckets, Fire Drill Bags, and Morale Kits. I will include how many of each item you may want to have as a general rule of thumb and the reasons why I have included these items on the list. So, here we go.

SCHOOL SUPPLIES

School supplies are the group of items that you will use the most as an educator. They are the bread and butter of the profession. For many educators, these items seem like something that they should have provided to them by the school district, but sadly many teachers end up having to pay for these items out of pocket. What many teachers do not know is that there is a good chance that their school district has many of these items stockedpiled in a warehouse. Having worked in multiple school districts in multiple states, as both as a teacher and an administrator, I know that many districts and/or schools maintain supplies of certain materials. The trick is knowing whom to ask for the supplies and how much to ask for.

In addition to knowing what and how much you will need, you also need to know how to conserve what you do have so you don't run out. Careful planning and some creativity can see you have a surplus of supplies to roll over to the next school year. This is a list of items I have found to be the most used and the most valuable in the classroom.

- **Pencils:** I personally issue each student ten pencils on the first day of school, the reason for this is so they can never say they do not have a pencil available. In addition to the pencils I issue, I always keep a large stockpile of these in my classroom as well. You can never have too many pencils in my opinion.
- **Pens:** Perfect for filling out those official documents and writing notes for students, I always keep at least three boxes of each color pen (blue, black, and red) in my cabinets and a box of each color pen in my desk. You should always be using pens unless told otherwise.
- **Erasers:** In addition to pencils, I issue one large eraser to each student on the first day of school. If your students are anything like mine, then they seem to either wear down their pencil's erasers quickly or break them off. I even had a seventh grader once eat several erasers. Don't ask me why. I also keep two spare boxes of the large erasers in my cabinet. When I taught smaller children, I also kept a supply of "fun style" erasers.
- **Correction fluid:** Two or three bottles of correction fluid can last you quite some time. It is great for fixing errors; however, you most likely will not use it that often.
- **Dry erase markers/erasers/board cleaner:** You want at least five boxes of dry erase markers. Every teacher knows that these markers dry out quickly and seem to get up and walk away after you leave your classroom. Keeping several boxes of mixed colors will ensure that you never need to ask your neighbor to borrow one. In addition,

I recommend keeping two spare erasers and two bottles of board cleaner with your extra markers. Put these somewhere secure because these things are like gold to teachers.
- **Glue:** Glue is an item that often dries out and hardens before a school year ends. Depending on if you use glue often for projects in your classroom, you may need several boxes or only a few bottles. I recommend four bottles or eight glue sticks if you use them only on occasion or ten bottles and twenty glue sticks if you use them often.
- **Notebooks and lined paper:** While most kids should provide their own paper, there are always those who cannot afford it or run out at the worst possible time. That is why I always keep either ten notebooks and/or four packs of lined paper in my storage area.
- **White printer paper:** White printer paper is even more rare and valuable than dry erase markers. If you can get your hands on reams of it, you feel like you've won the lottery. I keep as much of this stockpiled as I can. It can be used for projects, printing, and even bartering with other teachers. Yes, I have used it as currency.
- **Paperclips:** I always keep two boxes of both the large and small sizes with my supplies. I prefer paperclips to staples since they do not leave holes in the paper.
- **Staplers/staples/staple removers:** I recommend having two staplers (one at your desk and one in storage), four boxes of the correct size staples, and two staple removers. I recommend the staple removers that slide under the staple and pull the staple up instead of the kind with the four "teeth." They do less damage to the walls and seem to work much better.
- **Tape dispensers/tape:** I recommend having two tape dispensers (one at your desk and one in storage) and six boxes of tape in storage.
- **Pushpins:** Two boxes of fifty pins works well. I recommend the clear ones since you can use them anywhere and they do not stand out as much. Clear goes with everything.
- **Scissors:** I recommend having three pairs of adult scissors, one in your desk and two stored away. Scissors are another item that seems to just disappear from the classroom. If you have students use scissors a lot for projects, a dozen more of whatever size they will need is recommended.
- **Rulers/meter sticks:** I suggest having twenty rulers and four meter sticks in your classroom. I recommend the wooden ones since they are

more durable. Plastic rulers seem to break far too often. In addition, a dozen protractors are good to keep handy if you teach mathematics.

GEAR AND TOOLS

Gear and tools are a category of equipment I always recommend keeping in your classroom. These are items that you may not need often, but when you do need them, you will be glad to have them nearby. They are not the standard for teachers, but preppers often buck the trends of society and would rather have something and not need it then need it and not have it.

- **Multitool:** These are great for fixing small things on the fly. I keep these with me on the playground and on field trips. I once used mine to get a student's leg, which got stuck in a desk, out by disassembling the desk. Don't ask me how she got it stuck in a desk. It's one of life's mysteries.
- **Multiuse lubricant:** This lubricant is great for lubricating, removing rust, and removing grease and grime. It can even be used to start a fire.
- **Tool set:** I know what you are thinking. Didn't he just suggest a multitool? Yes, I did. A multitool is great for on the go or small projects. An actual tool set, however, is better for the big jobs like repairing desks and cabinets. I found it is often easier to do it myself then to hope for school/district maintenance personnel to arrive and do it for you. A hammer, screwdriver set, pliers, wrenches, hex keys, and a ratchet set are commonly used tools that I suggest having in your tool set.
- **Paracord/550 cord:** This is also known as survival rope. It has so many uses. I use it to hang items from the ceiling, as a clothing line for wet clothes on rainy days, for bundling items together, and so much more. Keep at least fifty feet of it in your room at all times.
- **Flashlights:** These are for when the power goes out or you need to look in the dark places under the furniture. Keep one in your desk and one in your storage area. A great alternative is a headlamp because they keep your hands free for whatever you need to do.
- **Lanterns:** Once again, these are for when the power goes out. I like the solar ones, personally. Keep two of these in your storage area and never worry about when the lights go out. Your room will be lit

enough for you to continue teaching while your neighbors sit in the dark twiddling their thumbs.
- **Duct tape:** Two rolls of this are a must. I have used it to fix student's shoes, rips in backpacks, and seal up boxes.
- **Electrical tape:** One roll of this is enough. It is great for cords that are starting to fray. Repair that power cord instead of buying a new one and save yourself some money.
- **Adhesive putty:** This is great for hanging up posters and other decorations. Adhesive putty is better than tape, pushpins, and staples because it is reusable and does little to no damage to the walls. I recommend two packs of this.
- **Sewing kit/safety pins:** A pocket-sized kit is great for when you rip your own clothes, and the safety pins are for when a student rips theirs.
- **Blankets:** If you live in a region where it gets cold in the winter, keeping two or three blankets stored away is a great way to keep warm, especially when the power goes out and the heat is off. If you are limited in terms of space, the emergency foil-like blankets are great and small enough to fit in a pocket.
- **Lighters:** Lighters have many uses. Keep two in your room, one in your desk and one in storage away from flammable/combustible items. I use them to melt plastics, burn fraying rope, and do other projects.
- **Tinder:** Tinder is lightweight material that easily catches fire. Wax wood, cotton balls soaked in petroleum jelly, or even dryer lint work great.
- **Charger/recharger:** For those times when your phone/tablet/laptop runs low on power. It is good to have a charger on hand. I like solar and hand crank–style units.
- **Resealable bags:** I suggest two boxes of both small and large bags. They come in handy for storing items and protecting your goods from getting wet on water day or field day.
- **Change of clothes/shoes:** Keep a spare outfit in case of spills, tears, or sweat. A spare pair of shoes are great for when a shoe breaks or you step in a puddle. Also, it allows you to change for a last-minute meeting so you look fresh and clean.
- **AM/FM radio:** A radio not only allows you to play music to soothe the "savage beasts," but also provides you with a means of gathering information during an emergency. I prefer the emergency radios that have built-in lights, phone chargers, and a crank so you can recharge it if the batteries die.

- **Batteries:** You should have eight spare batteries of each size you use in your classroom. AA and AAA are the most common.
- **Watch:** I always recommend that teachers wear a watch. Looking at your phone to see what time it is can lead to students taking out their phones. In addition, wall clocks need their batteries changed often. With a watch, you always know what time it is without the need of a cell phone.

CUSTODIAL/MAINTENANCE

You should keep the following list of items in your classroom to keep your classroom clean and prevent people from getting ill. Many of these items can be obtained from the custodial staff or parents may donate them to your classroom.

- **Trash bags:** You should always have a spare roll of trash bags that fit you classroom's trash can(s). I also keep a roll of large, durable trash bags handy. They make great smocks for art class and ponchos for rainy days.
- **Paper towels:** Keep six rolls of paper towels handy at all times. Kids spill everything from water to paint. If it can be spilled, there is at least one student in your class who will find a way to spill something all over the tables and floor. I always ask parents to donate a roll of these each year.
- **Facial tissues:** These are for when your kids get the sniffles. Keep several boxes of tissues handy, as they goes fast. Also, you should try and regulate their use. Some students will try to use an entire box in a single day. This is another item I ask parents to donate to the class. I have yet to have to buy a box myself.
- **Toilet paper:** Keeping two rolls of toilet paper around is great for bathroom emergencies, as well as for when you run out of facial tissues.
- **Disinfecting gel/spray/wipes:** I ask parents for tubs of these every school year. These disinfectants are perfect for cleaning off marker, paint, and germs. Keep several containers handy.
- **Broom/vacuum cleaner:** You need to keep the floors clean, and sometimes the custodial staff don't clean the floors as often as they should.

FIRST AID

If you are lucky, your school may already provide a first aid kit for your classroom. If this is the case, I always recommend looking through it to see if there is anything missing or that should be added. If you are not lucky enough to have a first aid kit assigned to you, it is easy enough to build a simple one for very little money. Having a good classroom first aid kit will reduce the need for you to send students to the nurse's office for small things that you can easily take care of yourself. The nurse will appreciate it, and it will keep the students in the classroom more. Here are the most common items you will need:

- **Container:** It doesn't matter if it is a hard- or soft-cased container as long as it is labeled, waterproof, and easily accessible. If it has compartments or straps to keep items organized, that is a bonus. I like to have it mounted on the wall for quick access, and it makes it easy for visitors to find it.
- **Adhesive bandages:** Three boxes of multiple-sized bandages will usually be enough to take care of all the little cuts and scrapes that children get.
- **Disinfectant creme/spray:** For cleaning up wounds before you place a bandage on them. I recommend having one in your first aid kit and either four tubes of creme or two of the spray bottles in storage. I also recommend one that has a pain reliever in it to help with pain management.
- **Latex gloves:** One box of whatever size glove fits your hands best. For those with a latex allergy, they make nonlatex gloves. These will protect against nasty bodily fluids or anything catchy your students might have.
- **Petroleum jelly:** I recommend one container in your first aid kit and one in storage. This is wonderful for minor cuts, scrapes, and burns. It also works on chapped lips and can be used for starting a fire in an emergency.
- **Burn creme:** One tube of burn creme is normally enough to keep in your classroom first aid kit. I recommend one with a pain reliever in it.
- **CPR mask:** This may seem like overkill, but you never know what diseases a student may have. There are disposable and reusable models available. Either will work.

- **Ibuprofen:** This is for the teacher and not the students. It is great for pain relief and fevers. I keep two large bottles of this in my classroom at all times. It is a lifesaver come parent–teacher conference time.
- **Stomach relief:** Keep a bottle or a box of tablets of this around for heartburn, indigestion, diarrhea, nausea, and gas. A school cafeteria meal has almost done me in more than once, and I was thankful for this stuff.
- **Tourniquet:** I like to keep an easy-to-apply tourniquet in my first aid kit in case of emergencies. I had a student who cut her leg badly with a broken toilet she tried to pick up (again, don't ask). I used my tourniquet to help stem the loss of blood until medical care could arrive.
- **Tweezers:** For pulling out splinters and thorns.
- **Student list:** This is a list of students, their medical conditions, and their allergies. This needs to be kept private and secured in the bag.

LOCKDOWN BUCKETS

A lockdown, for those who don't know, is an emergency procedure that is designed to prevent people and/or information from leaving the school grounds. In a lockdown scenario, the doors leading outside (hallway and classroom doors) are locked so that no one may enter or exit. Lockdowns normally occur when an event transpires on or near the campus and the school leadership believes that there may be a threat to the safety and security of the students and staff. This might be a dangerous criminal in the neighborhood, an active shooter on campus, or a natural disaster occurring in the vicinity. If a lockdown occurs you will need to keep everyone in the classroom without exception.

If you have never been in a lockdown, then consider yourself lucky. They can be either scary and confusing or boring and drawn out. There is often a lack of communication on why the school is being put on lockdown or how long it will last. I have been in several lockdowns and I can tell you that when you are locked into a room with three dozen students that must remain silent it is very uncomfortable. I have been in lockdowns that have lasted less than thirty minutes and I've been in a three-hour-long lockdown. When planning your supplies for a lockdown, you should plan for a six-hour-long period of being trapped with your students in a room without access to the cafeteria or a bathroom.

The lockdown bucket allows you to meet the basic needs of the students, on some small level, so you can make it until the lockdown is lifted. It allows you to feed, hydrate, and allow students to relieve themselves.

- **Five-gallon bucket with lid:** This item has two functions. First, it will hold all the lockdown items securely until they are needed. Second, it will serve as a makeshift toilet for the students and yourself. The lid will come in handy for preventing the smell of urine from stinking up the room and keeping it from spilling on the floor. This may sound disgusting, but in an emergency you do what you have to.
- **Shower curtain:** Hanging up a non-see-through curtain around the five-gallon bucket will give those going to the bathroom some privacy.
- **Toilet paper:** I don't think I need to explain this item.
- **Food:** I recommend gluten-free, salt-free, unflavored rice cakes. One or two for each student. These may not sound appetizing (trust me, they aren't), but they are filling, take up little space, are long-lasting, and will not irritate students with food allergies.
- **Water:** A two-gallon jug of water will ensure that each child gets at least one cup of water to keep them from getting dehydrated.
- **Paper cups:** One for each student and yourself. Paper cups allow you to serve water without students needing to put their mouths on the water jug. Some students will have their own cups/water bottles, but you need to be ready in case they don't.
- **Black paper and duct tape:** This is for blacking out your windows. In an emergency, you might need to ensure that outsiders cannot see into your classroom. This is true during an active shooter situation. Placing black paper over the windows reduces student visibility.
- **Attendance roster:** This is an updated class list with the emergency contact phone numbers of your students.
- **Emergency procedures:** A list of the emergency procedures that your school has in place, as well as your own procedures. Sometimes, when in an emergency situation, people panic and need to be reminded of the steps they need to take.

FIRE DRILL BAGS

It is likely you have never heard of the fire drill bag. I had never heard of it either until I came up with the idea of having one in my classroom during my first year of teaching. After my first fire drill of the school year (we had them monthly), I found that there were certain items I wish I had during the drills, and also if there ever was a real fire in the school, I wanted to have a bag I could hang next to the door that included items that made fire drills easier and more manageable. So I bought a cheap backpack and put together my first bag. It was so popular that by the end of the year, the entire middle school had asked me to build them similar bags.

The key aspect of the bag is the flagpole. Most schools require teachers to gather their students at a designated location, line them up, take attendance, and hold up a green card or red card based on if every one of the students is accounted for. In this bag, you will have a telescoping rod that you will attach either a small green or red flag. That way you can focus on your students rather than standing around waiting for someone to check your card's color. Here are the items I recommend for your bag.

- **Backpack:** This does not need to be a high-end, expensive tactical bag. An inexpensive, brightly colored backpack works just fine for this project. Use a pushpin to pin it to the wall next to the door, and you or a student can easily pull it off the wall when you need it.
- **Telescoping pole/rod:** You will need one of these to act as a flagpole. You can either plant it in the ground or have a student hold it for you.
- **Green and red flags:** These can be bought or made out of whatever materials you have available. They should be large enough to be seen from about twenty-five yards away.
- **Burn creme/petroleum jelly:** For if there is a real fire and you don't have a first aid kit available. I recommend one with a painkiller in it.
- **Adhesive bandages:** It seems like every time you take students out for a fire drill, someone ends up cutting themselves. One box of bandages of various sizes is usually enough.
- **Alcohol wipes:** For cleaning cuts before you put on bandages. Twenty of these will normally last you for quite some time and take up very little space.
- **Attendance roster:** Updated regularly to ensure accuracy. It should include contact numbers for your students.
- **Clipboard with pen:** For taking attendance and making notes.
- **Misting spray bottle and water:** This is for if you live in an area where it gets hot outside. Having a spray bottle with some water

can help keep you and your students cool while you wait for the "all-clear" announcement.

MORALE KITS

Being a teacher is one of the most rewarding professions anyone can choose to work in. Teaching gives individuals an opportunity to make a huge and lasting impact on future generations. It is also extremely difficult profession that is physically and emotionally draining at times. Those individuals that like to use the old adage "those who can't, teach" have never tried to teach a class of thirty-six students the Bill of Rights or a room full of teenagers about sexual reproduction. In truth, being a teacher takes a great amount of patience, dedication, passion, and the ability to do a lot with very little.

It is because of the strain that teaching can have on an educator that I suggest having a morale kit in the classroom. It is designed to help teachers get through the day. Especially through tough days when it seems like nothing is going right and the hands on the clock appear to be going in reverse. These are just some suggestions. Everyone has their own things in life that make them happy or relaxes them.

- **Candy:** Have you ever noticed that even a small piece of candy can brighten your day? I keep a small bag of hard candies in my desk. I've found that sucking on one discretely can help get me through a tough lesson or a staff meeting that seems to have no end in sight.
- **Favorite scent:** Most people have a scent that they love and makes them feel relaxed and comforted. For me it is vanilla. A candle or air freshener of your favorite scent can make the classroom seem more calming during a stressful moment.
- **Snacks:** Who doesn't need a pick-me-up every now and then. A small snack can give you a burst of energy and help get you through until lunch or the end of the day. Trail mix, jerky, and nuts come in small packs and stay fresh for long periods of time after their packaging is opened, and some can even be resealed.
- **Caffeine:** Boy do I love my coffee. I keep a coffee maker in my classroom so I can sip on my "life's juice" throughout the day. If you are not allowed to have one, however, there are caffeinated candies that taste like coffee that can get you through until your next coffee run in the teacher's lounge.

- **Backup lunch:** We have all had those days where we have forgotten our lunch at home. You can't or won't get food from the cafeteria, and leaving campus may not be an option. I recommend keeping at least two backup meals in your classroom—food that needs little preparation and can be stored for long periods of time.
- **Book/music/movie:** When the kids leave the room and you have a few moments to yourself, sometimes it is nice to have a bit of entertainment to help you unwind. I love to read and listen to music. Sometimes I'll watch a movie while I work if I have the time.

Note: When it comes to supplies, you do not need to spend a lot of money. There are many ways to cut costs as a teacher. You can ask for donations, request supplies from the school district, shop at thrift stores, and look at yard sales. I have even found organizations that will donate to teachers or have programs that provide supplies at reduced prices. What I am trying to say is that prepping does not need to be expensive. Always remember that you do not need to buy everything all at once. Most preppers buy just a little bit here and there. Throughout time, the supplies will start to stack up and you'll find yourself in possession of a hoard of much-sought-after goods in no time at all.

Chapter 3

Emergency Procedures

Knowing how to react during an emergency can save your life and the lives of those around you. When an emergency unfolds on your school's campus or in the vicinity of it, knowing how to react and being able to react in an instant can mean the difference between life and death. Many people think they know how they will react in an emergency. They have seen television shows and movies where the hero steps up and saves the day. They picture themselves in that role of the gallant hero. However, people do not often act as they think they will when that final moment comes. I know this because I've seen it firsthand.

In the military, soldiers (marines, airmen, and sailors) train for years on how to react when a dangerous situation arises. They practice and rehearse until their reactions become rote memory. Many of them get to the point that their reactions are more instinctive than a conscious decision. In regard to emergency procedures, preppers often practice their routines and procedures regularly until their reactions become second nature to them. As a teacher, who is responsible for the safety and welfare of their students, you need to be ready to make decisions at a moment's notice. They need to be second nature to you. Even if you are scared when the moment arises, you need to be able to react.

The most effective way of doing this is to practice your routines. Practice them with your classes, your colleagues, and also by yourself. Make changes to the scenarios you run so that the original plan you have in place cannot be used and you are forced to enact an alternative plan of action.

Thinking like a prepper means that you have backup plans for your backup plans. Being a prepper means being able to think on your feet and adapt to new situations as they arise. Unfortunately, many of the staff and students, in most schools, get so used to the routines of the mandated drills that they practice monthly, that they are unable to adapt when the unexpected occurs. When their primary escape route is blocked off or the fire starts in their classroom, they become confused and indecisive. Preppers are always testing their emergency procedure to find the cracks in their plans and then find ways to overcome these obstacles.

In this chapter we will look at how to enhance your emergency procedures for fires, lockdowns, and active shooters. Please note that your school district probably already has mandatory procedures that you are expected to follow. This chapter will focus on enhancing your ability to handle each situation and help you design backup plans for contingencies that your school district may not have thought of.

Something for you to think about is that the people who created the plans that we all follow during a drill, probably, only came up with the bare minimum requirements set by the state or federal government. Often they come up with only one way of doing things because they think that it will cover most situations. This is a dangerous way of thinking. Imagine if law enforcement or the military only did things one way because it covers most contingencies, we'd still have troops lining up in columns and rows marching down the middle of battlefields.

FIRES

Every experienced teacher has seen the staple fire drill plan posted on the wall or door of their classroom. It consists of an 8.5 × 11 laminated map of the school. There is a line drawn on the map that goes from your classroom to the school's meeting location. This is the "cookie cutter" fire drill plan. Your school probably has a fire drill once each month, quarter maybe only once a semester to practice the plan. The problem with this is that you are demonstrating to your students that there is only one way to escape from the school. That there is only one way to do things in an emergency. In addition, after practicing this routine and taking this route over and over again you and your students start to feel bored and complacent with the plan. The drill no longer is about preparing you for an emergency, but instead it is now a loud annoyance that interrupts your lesson and forces the students to cover their ears and complain about the noise.

So what happens when something unexpected occurs during the fire? What do you do when the exit you have practiced going out of dozens of times is blocked off or the doors you use will not open for some reason? What happens when the fire is right outside your classroom door so you cannot even leave the room to get to the hallway? Most schools never discuss with or even train their staff on what to do in these circumstances. Some people may talk about it or even joke about it happening, but they rarely actively seek out answers and solutions to these very serious problems. They adopt the "it can't happen to us" mentality. So when the time comes and the unexpected happens, you and your students get burned. Possibly, quite literally you and your charges get burned.

So how can we prevent you and your students from getting hurt or dying in a fire if the fire decided not to follow the school's plan? There are a few techniques that we will cover that you can use to increase the odds of survival for your students and yourself in case of a fire. These techniques are the evolving alternative evacuation plan, alternative fire scenarios, and fire suppression and evacuation equipment. These techniques will help you to become more flexible and better able to adapt to the varied and ever changing danger that is fire.

As I mentioned earlier, most schools use the same style of evacuation plan and you are expected to follow the route out of your classroom toward the meeting location. But what happens when you cannot follow the usual route? As a prepper and an educator, you need to know every possible exit available to you from your classroom. Whether it is going the opposite way down the hallway, using an alternative set of stairs, or even going out the window, you need to be ready to change your course at the first signs of danger. That is why I practiced going different routes with my students on my own time. It takes only five minutes to run a fire drill on your own. Doing this once a month will only take about forty minutes out of your time the whole year but can make the difference between escape or a fiery death.

The evolving alternative evacuation plans differ from the standard fire drill that the majority of schools use because it allows you to make changes to the plan as the need arises. School districts believe that their approved fire drills will cover most scenarios. However, there are many types of fires and causes of fire. The students should know how to crawl toward the exits since we know that smoke rises. What if the smoke and fumes are thick in the hallway, do the students know that they can wet a piece of clothing and cover their nose and mouth with it to create a makeshift filter? What if the fire is blocking your only door? Do you have a way to break a window and get the students out that way? Do your students even know to touch a door before opening it to see if it is hot or where the fire extinguishers are?

Running alternative scenarios will keep both you and your students sharp and better prepared. If you really want to test your skills, after practicing different scenarios with your class the first few months, write each scenario down on a strip of paper and put it into a jar. In another jar put several "X" factors that could occur. Examples of these could be that the teacher is unconscious, a student has broken their leg, or the fire started in the classroom. Pull one slip of paper from each jar and have the students act accordingly. You may find that some students displaying some natural leadership skills during the drill while others may show you who can be a liability.

Finally, we have fire suppression and escape equipment. As mentioned in chapter 2, I recommend a fire drill bag. This bag has the basics for the standard fire drill. I also keep my first aid kit next to it so I can take both with me during an emergency. In fact, I have students assigned to grab the bag for me and carry them so I am free to monitor the students and keep them moving. In addition to the fire drill bag and first aid kit, I recommend keeping a small fire extinguisher in the classroom and a tool that can break window glass. The reasons for a fire extinguisher are obvious. In case of a fire in your classroom or if there is a fire in your path of escape you can put it out or suppress it enough to escape.

The window-breaking tool is for those times when you cannot leave the room for whatever reason. When your only escape is through the window of your classroom you need to be able to open it or break it out. If you need to do this, make sure the tool you have can do the job. Certain types of glass do not break easily while others have wire running through it. Figure out what kind you have and get the right tool for the job. Once the window is broken out, lay down one of your blankets and send the students out to safety. If you are on the second or third floor of the school, then keep a fire escape ladder or rope handy to help the students get out.

By integrating these three concepts into your emergency plans, hopefully you will not only feel more prepared, but you will be more prepared. You may also find that your students learn from you how to be better prepared and become preppers in their own right.

MEDICAL EMERGENCIES

Does it seem like everyday a student is coming up to you with a scrape, cut, or splinter somewhere on their body? They always want to go to the school nurse's office to have their booboos fixed. You probably know, as an educator, that some students seem to spend an awful lot of time in the nurse's office. In addition, you also may have noticed that the nurse's office can get busy sometimes and students may take a while to return. As a prepper and an educator, you should be prepared to take care of these little bumps and bruises that may occur on a daily basis so your student's miss as little class as possible.

That brings up the issue about what to do when the injuries are more severe? In this section, we will not be learning any life-saving techniques. As an educator, you should have already been certified in cardiopulmonary resuscitation (CPR) and the Heimlich maneuver. If you are not already certified, then you need to get certified. I would also highly recommend that you take a course in basic first aid. You can often get your school district to pay for these programs, but even if you cannot, it is still worth the investment of your own time and money to learn those skills.

In regard to medical prepping, chapter 2 has a list of items that are recommended for a basic classroom first aid kit. You will notice that it is simple and does not include things like a thermometer, defibrillator, or MRI scanner. There is a reason for this. You are probably not a licensed medical professional. If a student is sick, then send them to the nurse's office. You do not want to get sued by a parent because you "diagnosed" their child and were wrong. If a child is mildly to severely hurt, send them to the nurse or call for the nurse if you can't move the student. If it is really bad, you may need to call 911 immediately. If you do call them, let administration know immediately afterward so they can clear a path for the EMTs. However, if a child gets a small cut or scrape, then there is no real reason you should not be able to clean up the wound, put an adhesive bandage on it, and move the student on their way.

ACTIVE SHOOTER

This is probably the scariest scenario any educator can face. The moment that someone decides that they want to kill children, for whatever reason, and then actively goes to a school to commit the murder(s). It is a thought that most people could not even comprehend ever having. There are two sad truths when it comes to school shootings, mass shooting, and war in general. The first truth is that we live in a world where there are individuals capable of inflicting great harm on innocent people. The second truth is that people can (and quite possibly will) get hurt and even die when these tragedies happen. It is an almost inescapable truth. As a teacher and as a prepper you must come to understand that this sort of event may happen. The second truth that I mentioned is often the hardest for people to grasp and I know that it is a hard truth to accept, but it is important that you know this. In an active shooter situation, people will get hurt and possibly die. Ignorance and/or denial of this are the enemies of the truth. It is possible that being ignorant about the senseless violence that accompanies these events may help you sleep at night, but ignorance can get you and other people killed. Denial of a fact will not make that fact less true.

Many states currently require schools to implement active shooter response trainings. The idea behind these trainings is that the school's staff will be better prepared if a teacher's worst nightmare were to ever happen. Unfortunately, the states rarely dictate the response plans and the training content that they want the schools to follow. Most schools use one of two popular response options. These two popular options are the lockdown plan and the multiple options plan.

In the lockdown plan, staff and students stay locked in a fixed location and hide. They do this until the emergency has concluded and the all-clear is given. The multiple options plan is a flexible plan that allows the staff to choose from a variety of response options. These possible tactics include attempting to escape, engaging a shooter(s), or finding somewhere to hide. It is not for me to decide what will work best for you if you find yourself in this situation. What we will be focusing on in this section is how to enhance your security and possible increase your chances of survival. Let us look at how to enhance these two tactics.

The lockdown strategy is the most commonly chosen plan for active shooter situations. It is a plan that requires very little flexibility and ability to adapt to ever-changing factors. Even though the strategy is the most popular with school districts, it has its drawbacks. One of these negative drawbacks is the fact that staff members and students who are outside of the classroom or are outdoors at the time the lockdown is declared are left to fend for themselves. During the lockdown, staff members are told to immediately lock their doors and to not open them until the all-clear is given.

But, what do you do as the teacher when you hear a person on the other side of the door pounding and pleading for you to let them in? Leaving them out there can mean their death and opening the door exposes you and your students to the shooter(s). For all you know, the person begging you for help may be the shooter. When I was an assistant principal and ran the active school shooter drills, I often played the part of the shooter. I would go around trying to get into classrooms. More than once a staff member or student opened the door for me thinking I was a student when I used a fake child's voice. Once they opened the door, I let them know on the spot that they were all dead. It was a sobering message to give people and I took no joy in doing it, but one they needed to hear.

So how can you enhance your security during a lockdown? There are several tactics and tools you can have at your disposal to help increase your odds of survival during an active shooter event. I would start by blacking out the windows. That way the shooter cannot see inside the classroom. If they do not know that people are in the room, then they are less likely to waste their time trying to get in. Of course, you and the students will need to maintain silence for the deception to work.

The next, and easiest, way to reduce your chances of being a victim is to decrease the possibility of the classroom door being opened. If the door opens from the outside, them wrap your 550 cord around the doorknob and tie it to a heavy or bolted down object across the room. This makes it harder to force the door open by pulling on it. Then, place heavy pieces of furniture in front of the doorway. I personally keep wooden bookshelves by the door just for this reason. By placing heavy objects in their way, you increase the amount of time and effort needed to get inside. Even slowing down an attacker may give first responders enough time to arrive and eliminate the threat.

If the door opens from the inside, then make the door hard to open. Fill in the gaps around and under the door so that the door is jammed. Then barricade the door with heavy furniture. You can do this by placing top of a chair directly under the doorknob of the door if it has one. You will need to push the chair directly toward the door until the back legs of it are snug against the floor. Another option is to barricade it with heavy furniture. Do not just limit it to one piece. Use several large, heavy items to make it hard to push it open.

For those of you who like gadgets and gear like I do, there are a number of devices that can be used to secure doors and windows. I have tried a few out and observed a few being tested and have found that some are actually pretty good. For instance, there are metal shelves that can be slid over the automatic door closer and it prevents it from being opened. There are modern versions of the old wooden door barraged that you can have installed to prevent a door from being pushed or pulled open. There are even small devices that are meant to be slid under doors to stop them from being able to be moved. There are dozens of companies that make these types of devices and some of them can be made at home easily. Even childproofing devices can be used to prevent a door from being opened by an intruder.

Once the door(s) are secure, move the children to a safer location in the classroom. Keep students away from doors and windows. Squeeze them into cabinets and shut the doors. Put as many into a closet that locks as possible. Stack desks and table into a makeshift barricade. Will these barriers, prevent students from being shot? No. There is always a chance that a bullet will penetrate the barrier and hit a student. However, the barricades may stop or deflect a small caliber round. Larger caliber rounds will penetrate most barriers you can create out of the materials you'll find in a classroom, but being hidden will make it harder for the shooter to find and target your students.

Now you need to keep your students silent. Take their cell phones away from them and turn them off. This may seem odd, but the last thing you want are your students making phone calls, sending text, or posting on social media what is happening. You also do not want phones ringing in the classroom giving away your position. If the students have access to their devices then there is a good chance they will be letting their parents know that there is a shooter on campus. Parents will want to come to the school and protect their children. It's in their nature to do so. Parents showing up on campus will only create more problems and make the current problem worse. They either become targets themselves or they become someone the police have to try to control. The more police needed to keep parents back from the campus, the fewer police officers available to engage the shooter.

If you are lucky, your classroom will not be targeted or attacked and you will be spared the horrors that have befallen others. If you are spared, you should wait until all clearance is given before you unbarricade yourself. Even then, be aware of your surroundings. Unless you are told otherwise, wait until someone of authority physically comes to your door to have you release the students. Remember that many, if not all, of your students will be emotional and scared. It is important to let them know that they are okay, that it is okay to feel how they do, and that it is over.

If, however, your classroom has been breached and you and your students are attacked, then you have two options. You can either fight back or not. Some people are more likely than others to fight off an attacker. Most experienced hunters can tell you that a cornered animal is the most dangerous type of animal. It knows that it has nowhere to run to and it is fight or die time. It is the kill or be killed moment. When an animal is cornered, it knows it has nothing to lose and everything to gain so it will fight harder to survive.

Much like a cornered animal, good prepper knows that you never give up. Even when the end is in sight and you feel like there is no chance you will make it, you do not give up. A prepper strives to survive no matter the odds and no matter the obstacles. If your perimeter is breached, then you have nothing to lose by fighting back. You will not likely have a gun since it is illegal in most communities for anyone to have a firearm on school grounds, but there are other weapons at your disposal.

As a teacher, I kept a baseball bat behind my desk, partially because I love baseball and played it with the students at recess sometimes, but also for protection. A hammer, a pair of scissors, a multitool, or even a broken broom handle are weapons in the hands of a prepper. If you teach science and have chemicals handy, use them to protect yourself. Remember, you are not alone in this fight. Have students who can't be hidden throw books, wooden blocks, or any heavy object they can get their hands on. Have them grab sticks and table legs, and use them as improvised weapons. In World War I, homemade clubs were commonly used by soldiers raiding enemy trenches. Table legs with hobnails, bats wrapped in barbed wire, and even sticks with lead on the ends were wielded by soldiers. If it worked for them, it can work for you. It is better, in my opinion, to go down fighting for your life then to lay down and wait for death to come.

If you are attacked, you may have casualties. If this is the case, you may have to preform triage until medical personnel arrive. For those unfamiliar with the term, triage is when you decide the order of treatment of the wounded based on the seriousness of their wounds and the likelihood of their survival. Since you are not a medical professional, you should divide your students into three groups. The first should consist of those who are uninjured and are able to walk. The second should include those with mild to moderate injuries. These are people who can walk if need be. The final group should consist of moderately to severely wounded people—those individuals who should not be moved except by medical professionals and who will need the immediate assistance of first responders.

Once the all-clear is given, then you will take your students to the designated area and await further instructions. It is okay to be emotional, but remember that your students will be looking to you for guidance and strength. There will be a time to break down and cry, but right then this is not the time.

Now we will discuss the multioption plan. This plan is centered around the military survival ideology of evasion, resistance, and escape. In this model though, we will use the terms run, hide, and fight. This plan revolves around the idea that the lockdown option may not be available or that the shooter has breached the classroom defenses. If the students are outside, in the hallways, or in the cafeteria then lockdown procedures may not be a functional option. If this is the case, then the multioption plan may be your best choice.

Under this strategy, the staff and students run. They either run, hide, or fight or any combination of the three until they are safe. The idea is to give the individuals (staff and students) the choice on how they will respond and hopefully survive the events transpiring. Maybe the individual decides to run for the nearest fence or gate. Perhaps they decide to hop inside a trash hoping that the shooter won't look in there. They might decide to start throwing books and food at the aggressor to deter them or even possibly subdue them. What matters is they chose their own options.

There are some obviously serious downfalls with this strategy though. The key problem is what if the individual makes the wrong decision or even worse freezes up and does nothing. Humans have a natural fight or flight response engrained within us.

Picture yourself walking down a dark, poorly lit alley at night. As you are walking, you will notice that your adrenaline is pumping which is making feel like you have extra energy. Halfway down the alley, someone jumps out from the shadows and shouts "Boo!" Most people will respond in one of two ways. They will either run away in terror or they will attack the individual. This is known as the fight or flight response. Most people respond this way to being frightened. However, even with this natural instinct inside of us, people still freeze up when startled. During an active shooter situation, freezing up may lead to death.

On the reverse side of freezing up is the chance of someone may make a poor decision. This could be because the individual is actually making a poor decision by choosing an action that makes no sense. It is also possible that the decision they made relied more on luck than common sense. Maybe the individual decided to attack the gunman, but they are so far away that the shooter has enough time to see them coming and reacting. Perhaps the student runs in the direction of the shooter because they cannot tell where the shots are coming from and they are just guessing. Maybe the individual is having thoughts of trying to be a hero and taking down the shooter. These are the inherent dangers of the multioption plan.

I cannot tell you what to do if this happens to you. The reason I cannot tell you what to do is because every school shooting has different factors. The number of shooters, the firearms used, where the shooting begins, and if there are any specific targets are all factors that will affect what you can and should do. In addition, your district may have specific guidelines it wants you to follow or training it has you to attend. The scary truth is that there may never be a right or wrong answer to a situation. There may not be a scenario or tactic that saves you and your students from harm. The sad reality of it is that sometimes the best you can hope for is that your decisions result in the fewest number of casualties possible.

The best advice anyone can give you is to be prepared as best you can. I recommend that you run through drills on your own and with your students. Let your administration know that you want school-wide drills or to at least have the autonomy to run drills for your class. Let them know that most police departments are willing to have their SWAT teams go through the school and help put together plans. I have had them do it for my schools twice before.

I also recommend that you help your students learn decision-making skills in stressful situations. I like to create simple exercises that I know the students can do, but add twists that cause various levels of stress. Time limits, changes to the rules or requirements, or add to the task. These help develop a student's ability to adapt to new situations and might help them to make split-second decisions when an emergency happens.

Chapter 4

Classroom Management

Now that we have the classroom set up, the supplies are being procured and stored securely, and emergency procedures are ready to be practiced, it is time to be ready to run your classroom from the moment the students walk through your classroom door on the first day of school. After all, what is the point of getting everything ready to have a smooth running classroom (or at least as smooth as a classroom can be) if the students are causing more chaos that is tolerable or safe. In all my years of working in education and in my many different capacities in that field, I have found that there is one skill set that separates the teachers that make it through their first five years from those who don't. That skill set is collectively known as classroom management.

What is classroom management exactly? There are many definitions out there for the term, but what it basically whittles down to is the ability of an educator to maintain a productive learning environment. To do this, educators need to have the same skills that preppers hone to ensure their survival. To a prepper, the ability to maintain order in chaos is paramount to their survival. It is the very goal that they strive to reach. To be able to do this, though, takes leadership skills, time management skills, and the ability to make the hard decisions. It is these skills that separate the prepared from the unprepared. These same skills are easily transferable to teaching career field and in turn classroom management.

When an educator effectively executes classroom management strategies, they create a classroom environment more geared toward effective learning. Classroom management skills help to minimize the behavioral issues that can prevent students from learning and make the environment an unsafe place. In my experience, some of the most effective teachers I have had the honor to work with tend to display strong classroom management skills. In this chapter, we will discuss some strategies that can help you manage a classroom or even a school effectively.

The best way to start this is by stating that there is no one correct way to manage a classroom. If I knew of one absolute perfect way to do it, that worked for every single educator, and was effective for every class of students in the world, then I would not only be the greatest teacher of all time, but I would be wealthy from selling that secret to all the educators of the world. Since I am not the greatest educator of all time and I am defiantly not wealthy, I obviously do not have the perfect solution to handling a classroom. However, throughout the years I have observed, tested, and learned certain techniques and strategies from the military, teaching, administering, and prepping that have helped me and other educators manage their students.

The topics that will be discussed in this chapter will be the mobile teacher, classroom rules, classroom procedures, teacher decorum, and a system of consequences. These areas of discussion will help a teacher think like a prepper and be more effective at keeping an orderly classroom.

THE MOBILE TEACHER

The mobile teacher is the core of my classroom management philosophy. It is the backbone of how my classroom stays so civil and efficient most of the time. The concept is actually quite simple really. I've learned that a teacher should be consistently moving about the room and keeping an eye on the students. It goes along with a prepper philosophy about being constantly vigilant for threats. The same philosophy is used in the military. You should always be vigilant. Preppers want to know what is going on so they can act at a moment's notice and, perhaps, head off threats or at least get a head start on them. As the educator, you are the sheepdog watching over your flock of students.

The mobile teacher walks around the room while teaching the class unless they are at the board. When they are at the board, they are regularly looking at the class to ensure they are on task. They angle themselves when they write on the board so they can keep an eye on the students. The mobile teacher lets the kids know that they are always being watched. A trick I used to help me keep an eye on students was to use mirrors and reflective surfaces to help me see them at all times.

I place small car mirrors at either end of the boards so even as I write, I can look up into the corner of the board and see the students. I placed some mirrors or items with reflective surfaces in every corner of the classroom as well. This let me watch my students without their knowing it. I once had my middle school students convinced for almost two weeks that could read their minds and that is how I knew what they were doing on their school-issued tablet computers. They finally figured out that I used the reflections off the cabinet glass to see their screens. They learned that I was always watching them and they didn't try to play games on them again in my class. After my first year of using reflective surfaces and mirrors, I had several of my colleagues mimicking my techniques.

The mobile teacher also moves swiftly and silently. They walk around among their pupils quietly so as not to disturb them. If they see a student off task they quietly react and get the student back on track. The mobile teacher is also very flexible because they are mobile. They do not need to have students get up to visit them at their desk, because they go to the student. The mobile teacher is far more effective than the teacher who sits behind their desk for most of the class and directs their students only from the front of the room. That's not to say that the teacher can't be at their desk if they need to be, but they spend more time on their feet than on the chair. The mobile teacher interacts with their class because they visit each students' desk two dozen times a day.

A huge benefit of being so mobile, beside the ones listed already, is that you get to visit with each student. Parents cannot complain that you are not paying attention to their child or that you have no idea what their child is doing. Since you are always moving, you are also having little meeting with each student. You can just say hello, comment on their outfit, or see how they are doing on a worksheet you assigned. You are all seeing and all knowing and that reduces behavioral issues and surprises about a student's academic level.

CLASSROOM RULES

There are many different philosophies in regard to the development of rules for the classroom. However, most of these philosophies can be broken down to two different camps of thought. The first philosophy is to a have clearly written out and well-developed set of classroom rules that cover almost every aspect of behavior. The other is to follow the prepper philosophy of KISS (Keep It Simple Stupid) and limit the classroom rules to a few simple ones that cover a wide range of behaviors. It is the latter philosophy that I personally agree with and follows the prepper mindset so that will be the focus on.

I remember hearing an old adage when I was younger that says that you should pick your battles. This is something my ex-wife would often remind me of over the years. This goes with the prepper philosophy because preppers do not want to have to fight or struggle when there is no need to do so. Why make your like more complicated or difficult than it already has to be? The idea of good classroom management is that it will reduce your stress levels over time. By deciding what is worth fighting students over and what is not, you will significantly reduce your stress.

When you sit down to write down your classroom rules that you will have posted, think about how many rules you are expecting them to be able to memorize. By setting long lists of very comprehensive rules, you may be creating more rules than you can enforce at any given time. I once worked for a school district that had a mandated list of classroom rules that were to be posted. There were around two dozen separate rules that the teachers were to have the students memorize.

Effective law enforcement officers know that there are a lot of laws but that they can't enforce them all. They keep this in mind when on duty. Think about every single law there is in your state and now add federal laws to that list. Now imagine your local police department trying to enforce everyone of those laws at all times. There are not enough police officers in the country or enough time in the day to handle all those possible law violations. Law enforcement officers could spend an entire day lecturing, writing tickets, or arrest every single person they see violating any law on the books. However, they instead focus on the laws that are more enforceable and important.

In my experience, when there are more than five to seven classroom rules, the students have a harder time adhering to them. I have found that limiting your rules to no more than seven rules is normally enough to cover all the important behaviors you expect to see from your students. The fewer number of rules that you have, the less there is for your students to memorize and they will be better able to focus on and remember the rules. It is very important that they know the rules in order to follow them. I ensure that the students can quote my rules on the spot by the end of the first day.

So you understand what I mean about keeping the rules simple, I have only two classroom rules.

1) Mr. Pierce is addressed as either "Mr. Pierce" or "Sir." Staff members are addressed similarly (ma'am, Miss, Mrs., etc.).
2) All students will act like ladies and/or gentlemen at all times.

These rules may not look like much but once they are explained to the students, they make a lot of sense. The first rule covers the treating of staff members with respect. There needs to be boundaries set up in advance. I know there are teachers who want to be the students' friend. I, however, do not. I am an adult and I do not hangout with minors. I also do not "friend" them or "follow" them on social media. This rule also helps to establish the fact that I am in charge of the classroom. Some students need to be reminded that they are not in command of the class. They are there to learn and I am there to teach.

This rule also teaches the students how to communicate with adults respectfully. When they get older, they will need to learn how to communicate with others and teaching them to address others by their honorifics or even as sir and ma'am will help them in their adult lives. Think about all the individuals you meet that you speak to respectfully for work. It is never too early to teach children to be polite and respectful.

The second rule sounds very broad I am sure, but once you explain what a lady and gentleman are, the students better understand what is expected. I explain to the students that a lady or gentleman is not someone who is wealthy, a noble/royal, or only in the upper echelons of society. A lady or gentleman is just someone who tries to make those people around them comfortable. I then explain how to do that by being polite, following school rules, and treating others with respect. Most my students understand this right off the bat with little to no additional explanation needed.

Because I use only two rules, it is easy to address students who violate one of these rules by saying "Are you addressing me the correct way?" or "Do you think you are acting like a gentleman/lady?" This way it is easier for students to think about if they violated one of the rules. They can then more easily reflect on their actions.

When you have fewer rules that are more general, you are more able to encompass a wide range of infractions with less wording. This is easier than writing down rules for all of the things students could possibly do wrong in an eight-hour school day. You should also make sure that you are stating your rules in a simple manner that everyone can understand. If you do this and regularly review your expectations with the students, then every student in your class should be able to immediately tell you, in their own words, what the rules mean. When your rules are made up of long sentences that require lots of thought and contemplation, you are hindering the student's ability to remember and apply the rules. That is not helpful to you or your pupils.

Finally, when deciding on your classroom rules, try to stay away from negative language. Words like "don't" and "shouldn't" set a negative tone in the classroom. These are words that should be used as warnings of dangers and not for everyday use. Try to phrase words in a positive way to show that following the rules is a positive thing to do. Here are some examples of possible classroom rules you may want to use. Always feel free to develop your own rules and always make sure your rules conform to your school district's policies.

1) Be respectful of each other and each other's property.
2) Be a team player.
3) Always help others.
4) Listen to the teacher and others.
5) Be the best you can be.
6) Be kind, courteous, and polite to others.

CLASSROOM PROCEDURES

Now that you have classroom rules, it is time to develop your classroom procedures. These are the procedures that students will follow when they are in your classroom or anywhere else on the campus. Having procedures that are simple to understand and easy to follow will give the students a sense of routine which is important for children as well as adults. Think about your own routines and procedures at home or at work. Do you do the same things in the same order every morning? Most people do and these routines and procedures comfort us and give our lives a sense of order. And that is what prepping helps us to do. It allows us to bring some order to the chaos going on around us.

When you start to develop your procedures think about what you want the students to be able to do with few to no directions from you. For example, how should they enter the classroom every day? What should they do once they enter the room? This type of thinking will help you develop routines that will become second nature to the students quickly as long as to stick to your routines and procedures. Here is an example of the morning procedures I had for my students when I taught elementary school:

1) The students lined up immediately when the morning bell rang.
2) The students then walked in a straight line to the classroom and stopped outside the classroom door and waited for me to open it for them.
3) The students entered the room one at a time. (I greeted each one individually and made random compliments or comments to each of them.)
4) Upon entering, they went to their desk, took out everything they needed for the day from their backpacks, and then placed their bags in the backpack bins in the back of the room. Once in the bins, students could not go into their backpacks, again as I closed the lids on them. This also helped prevent theft.
5) Once the bags were stored, the students sat in their seats and waited for my morning greeting and any announcements I had.

I used this procedure for years and it only took about one to two weeks for students to get into the routine of doing this every morning like clockwork. It became a second nature to them to do this every day. Even when a student came in late, they knew to follow this routine after giving me their late pass.

You will find that establishing these routines cut down on you having to give instructions on what you want your pupils to do. You should start with your morning procedures or for older students, the procedure for entering your classroom. Remind them of the procedures the first two weeks and see how the students start to do them on their own from then on without any coaching needed. Once you have your morning/entry procedures established, you can work on the daily procedures for the various tasks they will perform in your class each day.

These would include what and when to take out materials for class, testing procedures, or how to go from your classroom to another location on campus. It can seem overwhelming sometimes to think of all the routines you will need to develop, but if you think about how many routines are basically the same, then you will see how few you need to develop. For example, if you teach elementary school and you can have the procedure for when you switch from one subject to another. For me, the students had one minute to put away their materials from the previous subject and take out their materials for the new subject.

Another technique I have found that helps make transitions smoother and keeps students from malingering and wasting precious time is setting time limits. As any educator can tell you, you never seem to have enough time in the school year to teach all the material you are required to cover plus the materials you want them to learn in addition to that. That is why you should avoid wasting time as much as possible. When people take their time doing simple tasks in a classroom, they are wasting time.

When you set time limits, be reasonable, but consistent. Taking out a textbook, notes, and something to write with should not take more than one minute. The amount of time a student has to get to the bathroom, use it, and return should be no more than five to seven minutes depending on the location of the restroom. If you are giving the class a time frame, give countdowns. If you gave them one minute, let them know when they have forty-five seconds left, then thirty seconds left, and then countdown from ten to zero at the very end.

When you start to develop your procedures for going from one location to another on campus, you might want to consider using landmarks as stopping points along the way. When I walk my students from one location to another, I like to have spots when the class knows to stop until I tell them to proceed. This allows me to ensure the class is walking quietly and keeping together. When I want the students to start walking again to the next stop, I give the command to do so. Within the first month, I have found that I no longer need to give directions on when and where to stop and start. The students look at me once they stop and I start using hand gestures to let them know what to do. By the end on the first quarter, when my class moved down a hallway, neither they nor I made a sound. It is kind of cool when I think about it.

Once your morning/entry procedures and your transition procedures are completed, then you can work on your end of day procedures and the other ones that occur less often. These include testing procedures and your fire drill/lockdown/active shooter procedures. When it comes to test procedures, I recommend that you implement procedures that will prepare them for state testing conditions. These could include moving their desks from groups to rows, having students cover answer sheets with scratch paper, and having a book to read quietly when they are done with their test so as not to disturb others.

Remember that your procedures should be explained to the students from the very first day of school. The students should be walked through them step by step at first. Then, slowly, you pull back the "handholding" aspects and let the students adopt and implement the procedures on their own. The idea of procedures is that they become second nature and make your life as a teacher easier.

TEACHER DECORUM

You have your expectations for your student's behavior and how they present themselves. You have set the tone with your rules and your procedures. Now it is time to show them what you expect thorough your appearance and behavior. I am in no way stating that you need to be a strict tyrant or be prim and proper. On the contrary. You can be yourself, but you just need to be the business professional version of yourself. Remember that you set the tone of the class. The students don't only look to you to set the standards but also to maintain the standards you have set for them.

If you expect the students to be clean, wear deodorant, and not wear a gallon of perfume/body spray, then you need to meet those same standards. If you do not want to see the students wearing certain clothing or accessories, then you need to also not wear them. The same goes for cell phones. If the kids cannot play on their phones, then neither can you. Now if you are taking a call for work or something important, that is one thing. However, if you are just checking text messages or playing a game, you shouldn't be on your phone.

I like to present myself as though I am at a business meeting. I stand up tall, I am washed, shaved, beard trimmed, and wearing clean clothing. That isn't to say I haven't had my off day where my shoes are not shined or that I didn't get to shave in the morning, but I try to make these days the exception rather than the norm.

In regard to your attitude, that is completely up to you. I do recommend that you try not to act like a child in front of your students. When I say acting like a child, I mean name calling, having tantrums, pouting, and emotional outbursts. Try to behave like an adult. Speak properly and clearly and address your students respectfully. If you feel yourself getting angry or frustrated, try to rein it in and not lash out toward your students.

Basically, in regard to teacher decorum, you should project the image you want to show the world and that you expect from your students. We, as educators, want to be seen as professionals and therefore should act like professionals. Imagine a lawyer who shows up to court unbathed, wearing dirty clothing, and having a hissy fit. Would you consider their appearance and behavior acceptable for a professional?

SYSTEM OF CONSEQUENCES

So now your students know what is expected of them and what the rules are. What do you do if students do not live up to your expectations? What do you do if a student decides to challenge your authority? You need to have a plan on how to deal with these possibilities and more if they arise.

As an adult you know that we live in a world with rewards and consequences. You understand that there are rules and laws that we all must follow every day to be productive members of society (even if we think certain rules are ridiculous). Students, as developing human beings, need to understand this too. That is why having a systems of consequences is important for their growth.

Before starting to develop your consequences, you need to break up the types of rule violations into five different levels. Preppers, law enforcement, and military personnel use a similar technique to decide the level of force they can/should use when dealing with an individual. To simplify these levels we will use the term "Green Level, Yellow Level, Orange Level, Red Level, and Black Level."

The Green Level offenses are behaviors that are often low level in intensity. They can be passive in nature and are considered nonthreatening or are normally first-time, minor offense. The commission of this type of offense will not lead to the removal of the student from classroom instruction. In addition, it is the classroom teacher that will determine the appropriate consequences.

These offenses might include a minor dress code violation, not standing in a straight and quiet line, quietly talking with others, or being off task. These are offenses that normally require a gentle reminder to follow the expectations you have for them. The offenses are not causing harm to the class and are not laying a foundation for a pattern of negative behavior. If a student repeatedly commits a Green Level offense, then the student's actions would be upgraded to a Yellow Level offense.

The Yellow Level offenses are behaviors that are repetitive and may be escalating disruptions. These behaviors will not require the removal of the student from the school but may include removal from the student's classroom for a short period of time. Yellow Level offenses may include tardiness, the use of verbal or nonverbal insults, failure to follow directions, rude noises, or failure to stay seated when told to do so. Yellow Level offenses may also include Green Level offenses that are being purposely repeated.

Orange Level offenses are often behaviors that are chronic in nature. These behaviors significantly interfere with the safety, well-being, and/or learning of the other students in the classroom. These behaviors may also be of a threatening or harmful nature. There is also the possibility that the actions of the student are illegal. Orange Level offense often warrants the involvement of the school's administration or at the very least them being informed. Orange Level violations often include the removal of the student from the classroom or school on the first offense. This is especially true if it is a safety or security-related behavior.

Orange Levels offenses include profanity, pornography, and seriously disruptive behavior. Orange Level offenses also include cheating on examinations and assignments, plagiarism, and forgery of a parent/guardian's signature. These offenses will need to be reported to the school's administration and/or the school's disciplinary committee. The school's leadership team will normally decide the consequences for the offending student.

Red Level offenses are student behaviors that seriously affect the classroom learning environment. The behavior may seriously affect the safety and/or security of the student(s) and staff members. The offense violates not only school policy, but most likely is a legal violation. The commission of a Red Level offense may include extended suspension, expulsion, and/or a referral to the local law enforcement agency.

Red Level offenses include fighting, bullying, and aggressive behavior. The stealing of minor items or being in possession of stolen property are on the same level. In addition to those mentioned earlier, possession of tobacco, alcohol, gambling, possession of a knife with a blade smaller than three inches, trespassing, or pulling a false fire alarm are also Red Level offenses.

Black Level offenses are the most severe of offenses. These are the worst acts a student could commit on school grounds. These include possession or use of a firearm, explosive device, knife with a blade over three inches, or any other deadly weapon. Also included with this category is moderate to major theft, extortion, and the possession and/or distribution of a controlled substance. All of these offenses require immediate contact with the school administration and local law enforcement.

Now that the levels have been defined, let us look at possible consequences. You need to remember that students will misbehave in class from time to time. It is inevitable that you will have to issue a consequence to a student. As teachers, we might not be able to prevent all forms of misbehavior before they start, but we have ability to control our own reactions to student's actions. That is why we must choose our responses very wisely.

We must make sure that our responses are both appropriate and logical. When I plan my consequences for the school year, I try to use the old adage, "let the punishment fit the crime." This works very well in a classroom setting. When you choose a consequence that is illogical, then the students will not learn from their mistakes. Instead, the students will learn that you just react and give out consequences without thinking.

For example, while you are giving a math lesson, a student does not raise their hand. Instead, the student just calls out the answer instead. An appropriate response would be for the teacher to not respond to the student who yelled out. Instead, the teacher calls on someone else and after getting the answer, the teacher reminds the class of the expectations for raising their hands. If the student persist in just blurting out answers, then the teacher speaks to the student one on one. An inappropriate response would be for the teacher to allow the students to answer without having to raise their hands.

Another inappropriate response would be to yell at the student in front of the other students.

Here is a list of possible consequences for each level. You should check with your school's administration and the school district before deciding on a system of consequences for your classroom.

GREEN LEVEL

- Give "the teacher look."
- Move into close proximity of the student.
- Use nonverbal gestures.
- Say the student's name.
- Praise other students for making the right choices.
- Redirect verbally (privately, if possible).
- Tap the student's desk/chair.

YELLOW LEVEL

- Redirect verbally.
- Counsel verbally.
- Change the student's seat (temporarily).
- Give a brief timeout (isolation desk).
- Take away free time (recess/lunch).

ORANGE LEVEL

- Make a permanent seating change.
- Take away free time.
- Give detention.
- Take away points.
- Assign a lower grade (via participation points).
- Take away privileges.
- Issue an office referral (maximum).

RED LEVEL

- Refer the student to the school counselor.
- Refer the student to school administration.
- Suspend the student from class.
- Schedule a meeting with parents.
- Have the student sign a behavior contract.
- Revoke privileges.
- Refer the student to the disciplinary committee.

BLACK LEVEL

- Refer the student to school administration.
- Contact law enforcement.

These consequences are only suggestions. You should check with your school or district administration to ensure your consequences meet with district guidelines.

Chapter 5

The Substitute

Every teacher needs a substitute at some point in their career. It is inevitable that something is going to pop up that will prevent you from teaching. Whether it is an illness like flu, a mental health issue like exhaustion, a training workshop, or a personal errand like meeting with the IRS to explain how you could afford that yacht you just paid for in cash. The point is, we all miss work at some point and, therefore, we need to have a plan in place for when this happens. Being a prepper means being prepared for most situations including illness and events. You need to have a plan for whoever is covering your class. Just because you are unable (or unwilling) to attend to your students does not mean that the students will not show up and expect to be taught.

PLANS

There are three philosophies when it comes to being prepared for being unable to attend work. Of these philosophies only one reflects the prepper mindset; however, I will present the three most common ones. These philosophies are the "Not My Problem" philosophy, the "Throw Something Together" strategy, and the "I Am Prepared" method. These are the most common approaches I have seen taken by teachers throughout the years in my time as an educator. I am not saying that any one philosophy is wrong, but there are defiantly some major negatives with the first two philosophies that will affect not only you, but also your teammates.

The first philosophy is by far the worst of the three and I strongly discourage anyone from purposely practicing it. The "Not My Problem" philosophy focuses on the belief that since you are unable to go to work, that it is someone else's problem to figure out what to do with your students. This philosophy is common in noneducational career fields where others are often assigned to take your place and they know how to perform your tasks. For example, if you are a waitress, then another waitress can take your missed shift and she knows how to take orders, serve the food, and work the cash register. This works fine in other career fields, but not in teaching.

As a teacher, you and you alone know what you have taught to your students and what you need to teach them next. If another teacher just walked into the room with no idea what you have taught the students, then they would either have to start from the beginning or muddle through teaching the students what the substitute thinks they should learn. That will only lead to problems for you upon your return and set you back at least a day in teaching the students what they need to know by the end of the year. This philosophy will also garner you no friends and only irritate those individuals who end up covering you class. Avoid this at all costs or you will struggle to get substitutes to cover for you.

The second philosophy is the "Throw Something Together" strategy. This technique will require you to quickly put together lessons and assignments for your students with little time to ensure the quality of the work. While this method may be necessary at times, it is also stressful for you as a teacher. Often you will be doing this while sick or trying to prepare for the event you are attending. While this philosophy is better than the "Not My Problem" one, it still has its setbacks.

In addition to the aforementioned stress, there is the fact that you are most likely not judging the time or difficulty of the work you are assigning your students. I know that every teacher has crafted an assignment and thought they knew how long it would take. When they finally teach the material and have the students do the work, the amount of time you allotted seems off. Either the kids are flying through the activity and you will have time you need to fill or they are struggling with the material and you need more time than you thought. Now imagine you are a substitute teacher with this problem and you have to figure out a solution. Even worse, you are a substitute teacher trying to find a solution and you do not know the content being taught.

Rushing through a plan will not be helpful. Often when teachers try to throw together a lesson, they come up with busy work. While busy work can be nice for a substitute who has no idea what to teach, it does not help prepare your students or keep them on track for their goals at the end of the year. In addition, if you need copies made, you can never be sure that they can be made in time. It is better to have prearranged lesson that have been thought through and take your student's learning styles into account which leads us to the third philosophy.

The final philosophy is the "I Am Prepared" method. This is the more prepper-oriented method and the one that will bring you the most success. This method is great because you have a plan that is easy for the substitute to enact and developed with your students in mind. With this method, you will have premade substitute lesson plans and materials ready to go before the first day of school. Most people will undoubtedly say that it is impossible to always know in advance when you will be out. With this method, however, you will have premade plans ready for each month of the school year. That way no matter when you are out, you will be ready.

For this method, you will need to plan a set of simple lessons for a two-day period. The lessons will cover all the courses you teach if you are an elementary school teacher or for each class you teach if you are a secondary school teacher. The lessons should be preprinted, arranged in order, and placed in a marked container or location. That way if you call in sick, you only need to tell the administration where the lesson set is and they can give it to the substitute. These lesson packets should contain the following items:

1) A letter to the substitute
2) An updated class roaster
3) A daily schedule
4) Instructions for the assignments
5) The physical assignments

I always include a letter to the substitute covering my class. The reason for this is twofold. First, it lets you give the substitute teacher information about the class. Things that will help them be successful like the names of helpful, trustworthy students and which staff members they can consult for assistance. The second reason is so you can show your gratitude to them for covering your class. This may seem silly to some people, but by showing kindness to the substitute, you can increase the odds that they will cover for you again in the future.

As far as the assignments are concerned, I set up a box of assignments for each month based on what my long-range lesson plans look like. I then put them all in separate boxes labeled with a number. A bonus to having these is that if you teach the same grade level or subject every year, you can reuse the material from year to year. That way you are always prepared.

As far as the assignments go, I like to follow the KISS rule. I have found that a combination of a reading assignment along with handouts works great for most subjects. I try to include a video for some subjects as it is easy for the substitute to just hit play on the DVD player and a good video keeps the students engaged. Another great assignment you can give is an art project based on the subject matter. Have the students create posters or dioramas.

As stated before, I think that this method of being prepared is far more effective than the other philosophies. It requires a bit more work in the beginning of the school year, but yields great benefits in the long run. Knowing that if you get sick or something comes up and all you have to do is tell your administration with container to hand the substitute will bring you much relief, peace of mind, and maybe make you look good to your administration.

CHECK-INS

Some teachers are very protective of their classes and their classrooms, while others are more laissez-faire about their territory; however, any teacher who has had someone else use their classroom and returned to find that the room looks like it was just hit by a hurricane knows that their room and their supplies are very important to them. I know of instances where teachers have been out for a single day and returned to find that none of their assigned work was done and the classroom was a wreck. The substitute had allowed the students to use supplies that were earmarked for other projects and even gone through the teacher's desk.

This is not to say that all substitutes will allow this to happen, but the fact that it could happen should be enough for a prepper to be ready for such an occurrence. With this in mind, it may not be a bad idea to either check in on your class or have someone else do it for you to ensure you still have a classroom to return to. There are three ways to go about do this.

The first way is to have a school administrator check in on your class for you. Some administrators already do this for their teachers. They like to make sure that the class is putting their best foot forward for the guest teacher. When I was an administrator, I always checked in on the substitutes each period just to see if they needed any help. However, there are some administrators who are either too busy, don't think about it, or just don't want to check in on your class. That is why I rarely rely on administrators to check in on my class for me. Sometimes their schedules just don't allow for it and even if it does, they may have other things they'd rather be doing.

The second option is to check in on the class yourself. Obviously, it is not normally possible for you to go into work and visit your classroom even once let alone multiple times a day. However, there may be times when it is possible such as if you are in a training on your campus or near it. In those circumstances, you can always pop into your classroom and "just say hi" and make sure the substitute has everything they need or see if they have any questions. You can also just go to "pick up" something you left in your desk. Some substitutes may know what you are doing, but I am sure most of those would be glad for your presence to remind the kids of your expectations for their behavior.

You can also call in to your classroom and speak to the substitute that way. When I am sick, I will often call in twice to see if the substitute has any problems or questions about the assignments. You can also speak to the class over the phone's speaker, if you must, to remind the students about your expectations or explain an assignment you left for them. Remember the old adage, "If you want something done right, do it yourself."

The third option available to you, and the one that normally works best, is enlisting the help of another teacher or staff member to check in on your class. It could be a co-teacher, teacher's aide, counselor, or any other staff member that knows not only your students but also your expectations for them. Often the best person to choose is the teacher that neighbors your classroom as they are close enough to hear what is going on next door and close enough to just pop their head in to say "hi."

Whether it is you, an administrator, or a trusted coworker, it is important to ensure that your lessons are being followed and your expectations are being met. It may seem unfair that in most other fields, workers are not responsible for making sure their replacement (if they even need one) is doing the work correctly, but teaching is unlike any other field. As a teacher, you are responsible for the education of your students. You are the one who will be held accountable for any poor standardized test scores or district examinations that occur.

So you can see why it is important to be prepared with plans and materials for when you are absent. You need to ensure that not only your students are still learning when you are not there but also that you have a classroom and supplies to come back to. You don't want to get back from having the flu and find a classroom in shambles and a group of students that are behaving like something out of a postapocalypse novel.

Chapter 6

Getting to Work and Back

Every prepper knows that getting from one location to another in one piece is important. It is just common sense that if you attempt to go somewhere that you want to get there safe and sound. However, what people rarely think about are the troubles that can occur while in transit to their destinations. Preppers know that there is no such thing as a guaranteed smooth trip anywhere. It doesn't matter if it is walking down the street to the local convenience store or driving across the country on a vacation. At anytime and anywhere, trouble can strike. Being prepared for the types of situations that can occur is important if you want to be able to make it to your school and back home.

When considering your trips to and from work, a prepper needs to consider three things. The first is what method of transportation they are going to use to get to their target location. The second is to consider what route they are going to take to get to their destination. The final thing they need to consider is what gear they should bring along with them to increase the odds of reaching their target location.

METHODS OF TRANSPORTATION

So you need to leave to go to your school so you can begin a new day of educating and enlightening your students. The question is, how do you get there? If you are one of the lucky enough teachers that can afford an automobile, then maybe that is the best way for you to get to work. Perhaps you, like many teachers, are not paid enough to afford an automobile or at least not a reliable one. If this is the case, then do not worry or feel ashamed. There are many educators who cannot afford to buy a car due to having a low salary, student loans, or other financial restraints. Luckily there are other means of transportation available to educators. Even if you own an automobile, you may want to consider other options. Even if it is just for emergencies, to save a little money on gasoline, or reduce wear and tear on your vehicle.

The first option that I recommend is public transportation if it is available in your community. I have had to take public transportation more than a few time over the years to get to work. Subways and buses are options as are light rail systems. However, you need to understand that there are limitations with public transportation. Employee strikes, breakdowns, and large crowds can make using public transportation a hassle or not even a viable option for you. I recommend that if your primary means of transportation is one of these forms of public transportation that you have several backup plans available: there are a number of applications for your cell phone available that allow you to call upon drivers to take you to location if your bus breaks down. In addition, you may want to ensure that you know and are on good terms with someone who can drive you to work and/or back if the need arises.

For those who can afford it (and if you can please send me an application for your school district), you can take modes of transportation like taxis and ride-sharing companies. These provide you with transportation at, sometimes, a reasonable price. I once had an agreement with a driver that I would pay a flat fee every week to him if he took me to and from work every day. It worked out ok, but still the amount of money I had to pay each week started adding up. A cheaper version of this is school carpool. Some school districts can even help you set up a carpool if you are interested. I have worked in a few districts that have dedicated carpool initiatives that will help you find people near your home to ride with.

A third option is nonautomotive transportation. This includes bicycles, scooters (motorized or manual), roller skates, and even skateboards. I once worked with a teacher for a year who would come to work either on her skateboard or on rollerblades. The kids thought it was great and it was defiantly inexpensive and good for the environment. These options are also a great way to be flexible in your routes to work which we will cover later. I biked to work a few times myself for exercise and because in the spring 2009, gasoline prices were skyrocketing beyond what I could afford.

Walking, jogging, or running to school are also fine options if you live a reasonable distance away from your work and have the time to spare to make the trip. Personally, I chose not to live too close to where I work for security reasons. I know there are many educators who like living near their school and seeing their students outside of school hours. I, personally, do not want the students to know my address in case some of them want to play a prank or retaliate for a failing grade or discipline action I enacted.

In addition, I prefer not to see students in my free time since it omits what I can say or do when they are around. All it takes is one parent complaining that they saw you drinking whiskey like it was water and singing karaoke off key with your shirt off to get you in hot water with school leadership. I also recommend you only jog or run if your school has a shower available for you to use. Smelling worse than hormonal teenagers is not a goal to aspire to.

ROUTES

For most people, the route they take to work is the same every day. They take the same streets, make a stop at the same coffee shop, and park in the same parking spot at work. Their routine rarely varies. However, have you ever thought about the dangers that stem from being a creature of habit when it comes to the routes you take to and from work?

If you think about it from a purely security point of view, using the same route and performing the same tasks every day at around the same time is dangerous. If there are people who are looking to gain information on you or do you harm, then you are making it easier for them. This may sound like the ravings of a paranoid person, but you cannot deny that there are some dangerous and unstable people out there. It is a sad fact of life that there are people who would harm a teacher for something as petty as a poor mark on an assignment or because their child received a detention. There are plenty of other people who look for easy prey to rob, assault, rape, and even kill. With that in mind, you need to ensure your own safety and security.

A good example of how effective changing your routine is, is to think about how the military and law enforcement make regular changes to the routes than the personnel take and the times that they visit certain locations. While it might be nice that the local police officer always walks by a shopkeepers store at the same time every day, a potential criminal who is observing the store will know that the officer won't be close by later in the day since the officer is a creature of habit. In the military, personnel change their patrol route and routines regularly both stateside and when deployed. Keeping the enemy and potential threats off balance help to protect those brave men and women who help protect us every day.

To ensure your own security, think about having at least three different ways to and from work. They can be as simple as taking one or two streets over or going left out of your neighborhood instead of right sometimes. Also, think about leaving your home and work at different times. If you leave twenty minutes early or ten minutes later, you can be throwing off the plans of a potential attacker. In addition, it will keep people from being able to easily follow you. Finally, make sure you are always aware of your surroundings while in transit. If you see something that doesn't look right or that makes you uncomfortable, then you should do what you must to protect yourself. Never be afraid to call the police.

YOUR GEAR

Again, this is a prepper's favorite category. There are certain items a person should always have on them at all times when they leave the comfort and relative security of their own home. I will break this into three categories. The first will be the everyday carry (EDC) items, the vehicle kit, and finally the get home bag (GHB). Please remember that these lists are only examples. You should check the laws and regulations for where you live and work for what you can and cannot have.

Everyday Carry (EDC)

EDC. These are three letters that are very common on the internet these days. You see them used in everything from blogs to articles to even product descriptions on popular shopping websites. A person's EDC is exactly what it sounds like. It is the items that they have on their person at all times when they are not at home and sometimes even when they are. They are normally items that are small in size and can easily fit into a pocket. This list will consist of items many preppers consider to be essential EDC items. Such items as cell phones, wallets, and the like will not be on here since almost everyone carries these items already. This list also will not include any "weapons" since those are not allowed on most school grounds anyway.

- **Swiss army knife/multitool:** This is a must-have item for most preppers. One of these in your pocket can make a number of problems disappear.
- **Flashlight:** Carry a small, simple flashlight. While many people might laugh at the fact that preppers carry small flashlights in their pockets, they quickly stop laughing when they need help looking for something in the dark. No, the light on your cell phone does not count as a flashlight. Never tell a prepper that it does unless you are trying to make a joke.
- **Pen:** I recommend a "tactical" pen that can also be used for self-defense, but even a regular pen is better than nothing when you need to write something down quickly. Just be careful loaning it out.
- **Waterproof notepad:** You need something to take notes on with that pen I mentioned earlier. Waterproof notepads are great for when it rains or you spill your coffee on your pants/purse. They are durable and small enough to fit in most pant pockets.
- **Chapstick:** This is for when you have chapped lips, and it can also be used as a candle in an emergency.
- **Lighter:** This is not for smoking since most schools are tobacco-free zones, but for lighting or burning dozens of things, for example, 550 cord.
- **Cash:** Always keep at least $20.00 in cash on you at all times. I keep it in a separate part of my wallet so I do not spend it on accident. Small bills are best, but even a single $20 bill is better than having no money on you.
- **Coins:** I recommend carrying $1.00 in quarters. Believe it or not, pay phones still exist and can be useful if your cell phone dies.
- **Watch:** I love watches. As stated in chapter 2, wearing a watch keeps you from needing to use your cell phone to tell you what time it is. I prefer rugged solar watches. They can take a beating and keep going.

VEHICLE KIT

A vehicle kit is simply a set of tools and gear that can help you out of many common vehicle jams that pop up. I recommend one for each vehicle you have, but you can also have just one and move it from vehicle to vehicle depending on which one you are using. These are recommended item to have in addition to your spare tire and jack.

- **Container:** A sturdy toolbox or canvas bag works best.
- **Jumper cables:** A staple of any vehicle kit. I suggest checking your owner's manual to see what kind is recommended for your vehicle. I also recommend acquiring some that are between ten and twenty feet long.
- **Flashlight:** A sturdy flashlight with a flexible head works best.
- **Roadside flares:** Four flares will normally be enough to ensure your vehicle is seen by passersby.
- **Flat tire inflator:** These are great for that unexpected flat tire. If you are unable to change a tire or do not have a spare tire handy, this is a must-have item. It can get you back on the road until you find a tire shop.
- **No-spill gas can:** A 2- to 5-gallon can will help if you run out of gasoline on your trip.
- **Small toolkit:** It should include a few items, for example, screwdrivers, pliers, vise grips, an adjustable wrench, and a tire pressure gauge.
- **Car escape tool:** For cutting yourself out of a seatbelt or breaking a window for a quick escape. Keep this next to your driver's seat where it can be easily reached.
- **Duct tape:** For patching things up. It is a useful item to have.
- **Multiuse lubricant:** Great for lubricating and removing rust, grease, and grime. Can even be used to start a fire.
- **Permanent marker and paper:** For taking notes or making signs. Waterproof notepads work best, as you may need to write when it is raining.
- **Road map:** It is important to have a road map because you cannot rely on Global Positioning Systems (GPS) or cell phone applications to get you from one place to another.
- **Cell phone charger/power bank:** To keep your phone charged at all times. There's nothing worse than a dead cell phone when you need to call for help.

- **Emergency water:** A gallon of water is always recommended in case your car breaks down.
- **Emergency food:** Granola bars or other food that doesn't spoil easily. I like emergency ration bars myself. They last for years, and the flavor is tolerable.
- **Emergency blanket:** Either one of the foil-style blankets or a durable fabric one for when it gets cold or you need to sit on the ground.
- **Small foldable shovel:** To dig yourself out when your tire gets stuck in sand or mud. The old military style E-tools are great for vehicle kits.

GET HOME BAG (GHB)

What do you do when a terrorist attack, severe weather event, power grid failure, or zombie attack occurs and you need to get home sweet home? You need a get home bag (GHB). A GHB is basically a bag, like a backpack, that's preloaded with essential survival items that can help you on your journey home. These items include food, water, shelter, and a few small survival tools. This bag is meant to aid you in the event of a disaster where an evacuation is required and you need to get home.

In theory, a GHB should be able to sustain you for a trip of fifty miles that may take you up to forty-eight hours. Even though I am aware that under normal circumstances, it wouldn't take a person two days to get home from their school even if walking, you never know what events may transpire that may make your journey home anything but routine. This bag should be kept in your personal vehicle if you have one or in your classroom if you do not have a personal vehicle. It is meant to supplement your EDC gear. There may be repeated items on this list, but do not forget the old prepper adage: "Two is one and one is none."

Something else for you to think about is that in an emergency, if you are traveling home, especially on foot, you may not want to stand out. There are people out there that may out of desperation or some other reason attack you if they think you have something they want. If you have the ability to disappear into the crowds of people trying to get home and move about unnoticed, you make yourself less of a target. The idea that you can conceal yourself and the fact that you are prepared may be the difference between life and death.

- **Bag:** A sturdy backpack is highly recommended. I personally like military-style assault bags or messenger bags. They do not stand out, are inexpensive, and are very durable. If you have problems with your knees or back, or if you plan to carry a lot of gear, you may want a bag with a frame.
- **Clothing:** You should have a set of clothes designed for walking long distances. These should not be brightly colored or too tight. Think comfort and durability. I recommend a shirt, pants, two pairs of socks, clean underwear, and a zip-up jacket suitable for your climate conditions (if needed). Clothing that has been broken in is best, as brand new clothing draws people's attention. In addition, if you are worried about being attacked because of your gender or raped, then you might want to think about wearing less-feminine clothing.
- **Shoes:** A good pair of running shoes or hiking boots. The shoes should not draw attention to you or cause you to be a target for thieves. So no $200 sneakers or high-heels.
- **Hat:** A simple ball cap to protect your eyes, keep your head warm, and hide your face. The hat should not be flashy or block your vision.
- **Bandana:** A bandana is an amazing multipurpose item. It can be a scarf, a face mask, a tourniquet, and much more. Use nongang-related colors if possible.
- **Sunglasses:** A cheap pair of sunglasses can help hide your face and protect your eyes. Avoid sunglasses that you are worried about scratching up.
- **Gloves:** A pair of mechanic's gloves or leather work gloves are small, lightweight, and good for protecting your hands.
- **Face mask:** A small protective mask can be used to keep germs, blood, dust, or debris art of your lungs.
- **Pancho:** A small, lightweight item to keep you dry. Unlike an umbrella, it keeps your hands free.
- **Flashlight:** A small handheld flashlight with fresh batteries is a wonderful item to have on hand. If you also want to use it for self-defense, there are several companies that make heavy-duty flashlights that can also serve as clubs. No, the light on your phone does not count. A spare set of batteries is also recommended.
- **Lighter:** A small, inexpensive lighter can allow you to start a fire, burn the end of a rope so it does not fray, or even cook your food.
- **Tinder:** Lightweight material that easily catches fire. Wax wood, cotton balls soaked in petroleum jelly, or even dryer lint work great.

- **Rope or cordage:** As stated earlier, paracord/550 cord has so many uses. Twenty-five feet will normally be enough.
- **Multitool:** A small multitool can do a lot of things. It is like having a tool set in your pocket.
- **Knife:** A knife is a must-have survival item. It is invaluable as both a tool and a self-defense weapon.
- **Duct tape:** A small roll of duct tape can have many uses.
- **Small first aid kit:** A few bandages and gauze pads, lip balm, sunscreen, aspirin or ibuprofen, and antacids. If you wear glasses or contact lenses, you should include a backup pair.
- **Compass:** Even a small, button-sized compass can help you find your way home.
- **Food:** A few energy/protein bars are perfect for a GHB. It should include food that does not require cooking and that can be stored for long periods of time. Avoid anything that can melt.
- **Water:** One liter is a good amount for a short journey. If you live in a warm-weather climate, you may want to take more.
- **Water bottle:** A metallic water bottle is not only durable, but also it can be heated up over a fire to boil the water.
- **Toilet paper:** A small amount of toilet paper will bring you relief when it is time to go.
- **Solar charger/power bank:** A small device that will keep your cell phone charged.
- **Cash:** I recommend that you keep between $20 and $40 in small bills in your bag in case you need to buy supplies. In a situation where the power is out or the internet is down, cash is king.

Chapter 7

Recycle and Reuse

A prepper who can turn trash into treasure is a skilled prepper indeed. One thing that preppers know a lot about is recycling and reusing goods. Whether you are in an epidemic, zombie apocalypse, or just teaching Kindergarten, many of the things people consider to be trash today can and should be recycled and given a new lease on life. If you are looking to adopt some aspects of the prepper philosophy in regards to your teaching, then the practice of recycling and reusing are good to adopt. It will not only help the planet but save your money and give you more supplies to utilize in your classroom. We will break these down into plastic, metals, paper, and other items. I won't be covering organics, as it can be difficult to start a compost heap at a school.

PLASTICS

We live in a world where single-use plastics are one of the most common items found in landfills that can be recycled or reused. When most people think about plastic items that can be used again, they think about using plastic containers to hold various items. This is a great way to use old water bottles and other similar containers. The best part is that the clear versions of these containers allow you to see both the contents and the amounts that you have available; however, there are other uses for these useful items besides as a storage option. In this section we will cover water bottles (soda bottles can be used as well), milk jugs, and plastic bags (resealable and grocery bags).

When it comes to a water bottle, I am sure most of you are thinking about simply using them to hold liquids or small items. But there are other options. First, you can put your loose paracord into a dried-out water bottle. All you need to do is drill a hole in the cap that is slightly smaller than the width of the paracord. The hole allows you to pull the cord out without it getting tangled or knotted. You can also cut the water bottle in half and use the top half as a funnel. Since you still have the bottom half, you can use it as a cup. All you have to do is use your lighter to melt the sharp edges so you don't hurt your mouth. It also makes a great water cup for painting. A third option is to fill the water bottle with tap water, superglue the cap back on tightly, and place it in the freezer. Now you have a reusable icepack.

If you want to use the bottle for science class, you can turn it into a planter. All you need is soil, seeds, and a little water. Just place them on the windowsill and watch the plants grow along with your students. Speaking of gardening, you can make your bottle into a trowel. Just cut the bottle at an angle and use your lighter. Run the flame quickly over the plastic, and it will cause it to become more ridged. Now you have a gardening tool for digging. In addition to this, in an emergency, you can also turn a water bottle into a water purifier and even a trap for catching small fish. Moreover, you can make a tornado in a bottle by filling one bottle with water and food coloring and then taping the head to the head of an empty water bottle.

Perhaps you have some plastic milk jugs laying around the house and you want to find a use for them. In addition to the options for the previously mentioned water/soda bottlesx, you have more options with these larger jugs. Of course these make great planters and funnels, but there are more options available. The easiest way to use them is to turn them into book/file holders. All you need to do is cut the top off of the jug and then remove half of one of the sides. You now have a book organizer that holds most novels and children books easily.

Another option is to cut the bottom half off of the bottle and burn its sharp edges with your lighter. Now you have a bowl to eat your morning cereal out of. The size of the milk jugs makes them great weights when filled with sand. Perfect for door stops and keeping things from flying away in the wind like a tarp.

When you have plastic bags laying around the house, don't throw them out, reuse them like a prepper. One great way to reuse resealable bags, like sandwich bags, is as planters, just like with the plastic bottles. Resealable plastic bags, filled with water, and frozen are also good icepacks for injuries and headaches. Just make sure to double or triple bag the water to reduce the chance of leaks. Are you a messy eater or painter? A shopping bag can have the handle stretched and cut into half, then remove the other half of the bag. Now you have two bibs/paint smocks for small children. This works with trash bags too.

Shopping bags can also be used in a medical emergency as a tourniquet to reduce blood loss. It can be stretched out to make a cheap, plastic rope for tying small items together. Did a student step in something messy outside or is going outside and may step in mud? Plastic grocery bags make great shoe covers to protect your classroom floors from mud and other stuff kids seem to always step in. Don't forget, they can be turned into a rain hat by simply cutting it into half and wrapping it around the head like a bandana.

There are so many ways to reuse plastics in your classroom. I am sure you can even think of other ways and some great art projects to make using this reusable material.

METAL

So now you see how great plastic items are for increasing the resources available to a prepper. What about metal items like tin cans and aluminum containers. You have those leftover cans from dinner and those soda cans from your last party or from staying up to 3:00 a.m. grading papers. These can be as good as plastic materials. Metal containers are often stronger than their plastic counterparts, but can be harder to cut, manipulate, and over time can rust. The types of metals we will look at recycling and reusing are tin and aluminum cans. There are other metals out there in other forms you can reuse and repurpose, but these two are the most common and readily available.

When it comes to tin and aluminum cans, like soup and soda cans, there are several ways to repurpose them for your classroom. The easiest one is as pencil/marker/crayon containers. They also work great for paint brushes and the like. These containers won't get stained or ruined by the ink or paint. Anther use for a can is as a cutting tool. Once you remove one end of the can when you open it, it is normally quite sharp. These are like razor blades.

Want a gardening tool? Cut it into half at ninety degree angle and you have a trowel or scoop. Make two holes at the top of an open can and attach a string or wire to the holes. Now you have a small bucket. Want a cool, small lantern? Cut about a third out of the center of the can. Place a candle inside and light it. The polished inside will reflect the light. By doing the same thing, but drilling a few holes in the top of the can, you have a small stove for cooking. Similarly, you can turn a can into a mini fire barrel by drilling a few holes in the sides of the can. Now you have a way to keep warm outdoors.

PAPER

We have covered plastics and metals and now it is time to discuss what to do with all that paper you and your students throw out. Believe it or not, there are several great ways to reuse paper. For this section, we will cover the repurposing of cardboard, toilet paper/paper towel rolls, and sheets of paper.

When it comes to cardboard, most people think that all you can do with an old box is store items in them. However, you have plenty of other options available to you. First, you can take thin pieces of cardboard and spray paint them white. Next, you cut the cardboard into strips about two inches wide and four to five inches long. The kids can decorate the strips and they have great bookmarks they made themselves. Another option for you is that you can cut the cardboard into squares and use them as padding and barriers. Cardboard also makes great canvases for student artwork and projects including using them instead of buying project boards. Finally, you can use the cardboard as protective covering for your desks, tables, and floors. That way students can ruin them by spilling paint or getting ink on them from dropped markers.

Toilet paper and paper towel rolls can make great supplies for your classroom. Of course the potential art projects easily come to mind. There are so many creative art activities that you can do with your class. However, you can also use them for so much more. You can cover a roll in peanut butter, roll it in bird seed, and then hang it from a tree to make an inexpensive bird feeder. You can place the rolls and water into a blender and puree the mix until it is completely mixed. Pour the combination into a large bowl and then place another bowl into the first one. let it dry overnight and you have a homemade bowl you can decorate. You can place the tubes into an old shoebox. You now have a way to store colored pencils and markers by color.

You can fold in one side of a toilet paper roll and fill it three quarters of the way full with soil. Now you have a biodegradable planter. Place an old sock over the end of a roll. Dip the sock in bubble solution and you have a cool bubble blower. Mix egg shells, flour, food coloring and water into a sandwich bag. Mix the contents well. Place tape over one end of a roll and then pour the mix you made into the other end. Wait twenty-four hours and you will have some colored chalk rolls. Finally, you can take your rolled up power cords and slide the bundles into a roll and it will keep them from coming undone.

When it comes to sheets of paper, there are a few ways to easily reuse and repurpose them. First of all, you can use the unused back side of the papers as scratch paper. You can also use that blank side for faxes (yes, I know that using a fax machine dates me). Want some pocket-sized notebooks? Cut the unused sections of the paper off and staple them together to make cheap notebooks. Perhaps you want to come up with a fun project? Paper-mache is always a winner with students of all ages.

Here is a good one. Take used paper and have your students cut it into tiny pieces or use a shredder, place the pieces into a blender with water and puree. Pour the mixture onto an old windscreen and smooth it out. Let it dry for a few days and now you have new paper for projects. The best part is you can reuse this paper several times.

There are also some paper items that most people don't think to save that can be helpful for a teacher on a budget. Greeting cards can have the pictures removed and used for art collages or homemade notebook covers. Magazines are wonderful for collages as well as being wonderful for notebook dividers, and being folded into colorful envelopes. Newspaper can be used for paper-mache, pureed into new paper, and made into very creative wrapping paper. And let us not forget those stacks of magazine subscription cards. They make great bookmarks.

As you can see, there are many ways to reduce your waste, reuse items, and save your money all at the same time. It is important for a prepper to be able to adapt to situations as they arise and a lack of materials is defiantly a situation that will arise often in your tenure as a teacher. Being able to turn trash into treasure will be a life saver for the prepper that can think on their toes and be creative.

Chapter 8

Conclusion

A prepper is just a person who wants to be prepared for the difficulties in life that seem to creep up when you least expect them. I know that there are many people who think of preppers as "crazy" people who hoard food and supplies and have bunkers in their backyards. People think that the prepper community is made up of the paranoid, the delusional, and the most militaristic of society. But they couldn't be more wrong.

Preppers are just people, like you and me, who want to make it from day to day. They heard the story about the grasshopper and the ant when they were young and took the moral of the story to heart and never forgot it. It is easy to laugh, condemn, and even fear preppers. They are often the butt of jokes or the comedic relief in television and films. However, when things go wrong in an emergency, which they often do, who does everyone go running to for help? The people who were ready for the emergency.

As an educator, you are entrusted with one of the greatest resources in this world. The very future of humanity. The young people that you dedicate your life to educating and guiding through their developmental years need all the help they can get. It is your responsibility to provide them with the best education possible. This may seem like a lot of responsibility and it is. Yet, every year, millions of teachers throughout the world show that they are not only up to the challenge but can exceed the expectations set for them.

Unfortunately, as educators, we seldom have the tools at our disposal to do what we need to get the job done to the best of our ability. And when we do finally get our hands on those most holy and mythical of things we like to call teaching supplies, then we weep with joy. Oh yes, we weep. We weep because we know that those few scarps of supplies will only go so far and last only so long. After they are gone, you are more likely to get your hands on a motorcycle riding unicorn that plays electric guitar than a ream of paper or toner for the copy machine.

As a prepper you will hopefully be able to gather, store, and better utilize those precious resources you get your hands on. Just remember that preppers don't give up just because we don't have what we need. It is quite the opposite. Instead, preppers look around at what they do have to work with and start getting creative. A teacher that thinks like a prepper can turn a pile of junk into a veritable smorgasbord of learning materials.

Hopefully you will think about the topics covered in this book and start to plan for the future of your classroom and your student's educational and safety needs. Just start by gathering some supplies whenever you can here and there. You don't need to buy it all at once. Store away as much of your goods as you possibly can. If you work on this slowly and use the strategies shared in this book, you might end up making the hoarders you see on television look at you like you are the one with a problem. Remember to hide those most valuable of resources that are most dear to you and have a tremendous value on the teacher lounge black market.

One final thought for you to think about once you close this book: Teachers are important and valued members of society. Without teachers there would be no doctors, lawyers, or any other profession. Teachers provide the essential knowledge and skills that make those professions possible.

THE END.

About the Author

Donald J. Pierce has been an educator for more than twelve years. He has served as a teacher at the elementary, middle, and high school levels, and been a school administrator. He is also a U.S. Air Force veteran and a veteran of Operation Iraqi Freedom.

www.ingramcontent.com/pod-product-compliance
Lightning Source LLC
Chambersburg PA
CBHW032031230426
43671CB00005B/276